I LIE FOR MONEY

*Candid, Outrageous Stories from a
Magician's Misadventures*

STEVE SPILL

Skyhorse Publishing

Copyright © 2015 by Steve Spill/Magic Concepts, Inc

Skyhorse Publishing books may be purchased in bulk at special discounts for sales promotion, corporate gifts, fund-raising, or educational purposes. Special editions can also be created to specifications. For details, contact the Special Sales Department, Skyhorse Publishing, 307 West 36th Street, 11th Floor, New York, NY 10018 or info@skyhorsepublishing.com.

Skyhorse® and Skyhorse Publishing® are registered trademarks of Skyhorse Publishing, Inc.®, a Delaware corporation.

Visit our website at www.skyhorsepublishing.com.

10 9 8 7 6 5 4 3 2 1

Library of Congress Cataloging-in-Publication Data

Spill, Steve, 1955-
I lie for money : candid, outrageous stories from a magician's misadventures / Steve Spill.
    pages cm
   Summary: "In this funny, irreverent, unique, eccentric memoir, magician Steve Spill reveals how he managed to survive decades inside a rarely profitable, sometimes maddening, but often deliciously rewarding offbeat showbiz profession--magic!"-- Provided by publisher.
 ISBN 978-1-63220-492-9 (hardback) -- ISBN 978-1-63220-862-0 (ebook) 1. Spill, Steve, 1955- 2. Magicians--United States--Biography. I. Title.
 GV1545.S75A3 2015
 793.8092--dc23
                                    2015008849

Cover design by Rain Saukas
Cover photo credit Sal Taylor Kydd

ISBN: 978-1-63220-492-9
Ebook ISBN: 978-1-63220-862-0

Printed in the United States of America

Dedication

To each person that buys this book and encourages others to do the same; Adam and Irena Wrobel for having a daughter with a contagious zest for life named Bozena who makes my life make sense; to that daughter of course; my parents, Sandy and Shirley, for birthing me with the best of each of their qualities; boyhood magical mentors who added what was between their ears to what's between my ears; Bob Sheets for giving me my first best jobs; Penn & Teller for their generosity and inspiration; Asuka Hisa for engaging me to speak at the Santa Monica Museum of Art about my journey as a magician—the seed that grew into this book; Mark Miller for getting me to Julie Ganz at Skyhorse Publishing who shepherded the passage of my manuscript into book form; Magicopolis staff both past and present; and to anyone who has ever bought a ticket to one of my shows, I appreciate you all.

CONTENTS

PART FIVE: ODDS & ENDS

PART SIX: AND NOW A WORD FROM OUR SPONSOR

PART SEVEN: MAGICOPOLIS

Introduction

"It is very difficult for a magician to deceive intelligent people without prevaricating. So everything I say is not true; this is true or I would not tell you so."

Karl Germain, a master magician considered by his peers to be one of the finest that ever lived, uttered these words. Germain, who lived from 1878 to 1959, also famously said, "Conjuring is the only absolutely honest profession—a conjuror promises to deceive and he does."

Being the classy guy that he was, when Germain described the performing art of magic, he avoided the words "liar," "lying," and "lie." He also justified his deceptions for the sake of art, like the person who does a nude scene in a movie for the art of it (okay, maybe not *exactly* like that). Anyway, when not writing this book I am a magician who is proud to lie for my art, but I also do it to pay the mortgage. When I first started, I had only two dollars in my pocket, and look at me now, I owe thousands. I am a professional.

Other fact re-constructionists and reality stylists lie to their wives that there's no other woman, or lie to the other woman that they don't have a wife . . . or promise to pay you back out of their next paycheck, or tell you they're from the government and are here to help you. The magician is an extraordinary breed of liar. In fact, there's not another creature on earth that would lie to make you think a coin is in their left fist when it's really under the saltshaker.

Buried alive and living, transforming nubile young girls into savage tigers, floating humans, sawing women in two, vanishing elephants, appearing persons, mind reading, teleportation, time control, dangerous Houdini-inspired escapes, walking on water (actually, that one's not a big deal, if you know where the sand bars are)—each and every one of those feats are magicians' lies, designed to amuse audiences by making them feel their eyes are pairs of liars, and that their brains are lying to them too.

As you read this book you will question why any sane person would do some of the things I've done—like swallowing sewing needles, stabbing myself, having someone pull the trigger of a gun pointed at my face, or being chained to a metal table and allowing a burning rope to drop thirty-nine sharpened steel spikes on me from fifteen feet above. Because I've done this stuff doesn't mean you'll be able to do it. Even if you think you know how to do these things safely, you'd still be a bonehead to try them. Leave it to me. I'm an expert.

The trick of our trade is to alter perceptions with dyslexic displays of honesty that range from tiny little manipulative untruths to big, fat, in-your-face, lies. To be a professional magician is to be an expert at dispensing disinformation, duplicity, hypocrisy, distortion, deception, and fakery without any of the guilt or unpleasant consequences. And we enjoy the thrill of getting away with it. Many of the defects you were taught to avoid in childhood are the very qualities that become your virtues as a magician. True practitioners of the craft do the same sort of things up front and above board in the name of entertainment that most governments do secretly in the name of espionage.

There may be some performing arts better than magic, and some may be worse, but there is nothing exactly like it. In his book, *House of Mystery*, that genius of deception, Teller, wrote, "In real life, effects have causes. In good magic, effects have fake causes that are beautiful or funny or thought provoking. That's the idea of magic: connecting a cause with an effect by means of a lie that tells a greater truth." Doesn't that sound cool? Also from Teller, "When a magician lets you notice something on your own, his lie becomes impenetrable. Nothing fools you better than the lie you tell yourself."

Since performing magic is largely about lying, it makes sense that I'd be a magician; I've always largely loved to lie. In school I used to turn in book reports about books that didn't exist. Phony stories, fake authors, all made up by me. If a teacher questioned me about one of my bogus books, I'd say I got it at a swap meet, granny's garage, or it somehow mysteriously appeared on my doorstep.

Although my mind tells me I'm half my present age of sixty years, in reality I have spent better than fifty years, as man and boy, turning tricks. Yes, I've been a magician for a very long time. No, I did not go to high school with Harry Houdini. Nor do I have cloven hooves or wear a top hat to make room for my horns. My best work is probably still ahead of me, but herein lies the details of my long and mediocre career to date. The places I've been, the people I have met—from Santa Monica's beach sands and Adam Sandler to South Africa east of the Great Kei River and Joan Rivers—getting up in front of crowds, hanging out with celebrities, illiterates, intellectuals, jungle natives, insurance salesmen...

As a magician I have functioned at just about every known type of affair. I have run the gamut. I have performed the same day at a bon voyage party in San Pedro and at a circumcision in Oxnard (fortunately, I was able to do the same act at both occasions). What I am is a laborer, a worker, and what's written here chronicles achievements that have turned me into something less than a household name, but have made me a very happy man.

Even though I know you can't live in the past, it's nice to have one, and this book is a welcome opportunity to put into words the past that lives in me. My job has always been to make people see and experience things they cannot see and experience in their own lives. And despite all the money or accolades or whatever else being a magician brings you, there is nothing else, not a thing in the world, that can ever compare to making an audience happy. Even if you're atheist, you can't help, for that one brief moment, believing in God. The purpose of this book is the same, to spread joy and wonder and make you happy... OK, that wasn't entirely honest—I also hope to maybe make a few frogskins in the process.

This is not an unabridged autobiography. Although I've known me a long time and am well acquainted with myself,

I don't pretend to remember and assemble every important thing that happened to me until now. I best recollect certain bits and pieces, and of those my aim was to leave out all the boring stuff. One of the first lessons I learned as a magician was that the audience doesn't care how you feel; they care how they feel. If people wanted to see, or read for that matter, something that made them feel bad, hospitals could sell tickets. As I said when I broke my ankle onstage during a show in Chevy Chase, Maryland, "What ankle?" When you buy a ticket to see a performance, the entertainer owes you your money's worth. Same with a book, well, it is in my book.

Memory is like a fun house mirror. Its distortions reflect bad stuff in a thinner form than that in which it originally appeared, and good things in a wider aspect than they deserve. I've tried to beat down my vanity, but anyone who writes about himself is apt to fall into the magician's habit of peeking at the deck to find out where the aces lie. This tome is my fist full of aces. In other words, my life is an open book with a bunch of the pages stuck together; included are only what I consider the most surprising, relevant, interesting, or funny parts of my journey as a magician.

And by the way, I'm not above rearranging my experiences to improve a story, like when my shows absolutely sucked. If I told you that at times I was the worst magic act ever in the history of the world, I'd be lying—I wasn't that good. But when you're in love with what you're doing there's no shame in failing; you're resilient, you bounce back quickly from failures, you're always willing to take risks, and you don't put yourself down if something doesn't work out. I've usually managed to learn something from the defeats, but hardly anything from the victories.

Part of the reason I wrote this book was to share with those who wish to craft a self-directed creative life—be it an actor, painter, writer, comedian, magician, or whatever— and describe how one can survive in rarely profitable but rewarding professions. You may not become a bazillionaire, but you can be a winner. Nobody makes a living as a magician by accident. You gotta want it pretty bad. Success comes by enjoying the journey, hard work helps you improve, and when you're obsessed you make your luck. At the moment I am neither the best nor the worst magician, but perhaps the luckiest.

The important thing to know about me is that I lie a lot. That's the truth. But, usually, when I lie, I admit it. I'm a very honest liar who stole that terribly clever "Honest Liar" phrase, along with other ideas, from George Burns...making me not just a liar, but also a thief. Lying and remixing stolen bits and pieces of other's ideas isn't just for magicians; it's for everyone. Like David Bowie said, "The only art I'll ever study is stuff that I can steal from." The trick is to take a tiny bit from a lot of sources to create something new and different. But enough about stealing; the fact is, everything you've read in this paragraph is a lie, which proves what a truthful man I am. If I tell you something is a lie, you know it's the truth. But when I write about my life, I don't lie. I don't have to. The truth is unbelievable enough.

I USED TO OPEN FOR THE EAGLES, NOW STING IS OPENING FOR ME

I gave the audience the finger with both hands and disappeared. I was a proud nineteen-year-old magician and wasn't going to get booed without returning the insult. It was the first time in my young career that I learned what it felt like to really fail on stage. At the time I was unaware of any rock concerts, besides the ones I was doing, that had a magician as an opening act; maybe there was a reason for that? The unruly crowd booed so loud, it was unbearably embarrassing, and although you can't really die from embarrassment, it definitely can feel fatal. I'm still trying to forget that show when I opened for a band called Flash Cadillac and the Continental Kids at Colorado Springs Municipal Auditorium.

I had been a master opener in a plethora of rock nightclubs, so it was an easy matter in my mind to just chalk up my larger venue concert failure to the overcrowding and late start time. But apparently that wasn't it, because my next huge event didn't go any better. When I opened for Paul Revere and the Raiders at Bakersfield Civic Auditorium, the band's manager told me, "Your first talent isn't going to be comedy or magic, kid, it's going to be taking rejection—just don't let it get you down. You'll never see me letting rejection get me down. It might get me down, but I won't let anyone see it." I wanted to kick that manager in the nuts, but I didn't. From start to finish, the entire life span of my ill-fated Highdini act was a scant two years.

Most of you have never heard of me. My name is Steve Spill, and I am a magician who is very well known to those who know me, and completely unknown to those who have never heard of me. Those who know me are other professional magicians, a few fans, and some residents of Santa Monica, California, where I've been producing and performing magic shows since 1998, in a theater I designed, built, run, and named, Magicopolis. Producing and performing magic shows was nothing new to me in 1998, but designing, building, and running a theater were.

As a lifelong magician, one of my desires in terms of the design and build was that every person in the audience could see me from head to toe at every moment, and ideally that I could see each and every face in the crowd. Too many times I'd worked venues where people seated beyond the first row only saw me from the waist up. And I wanted the spectators really close, so even from the furthest seat from the stage a coin or the face of a card would be clearly visible.

Flash-forward fifteen years, to November 5, 2013, and last night Sting was my opening act at Magicopolis. When I say Sting, I mean THE Sting, the sixteen-time Grammy Award-winning musician. He performed songs from his new album, *The Last Ship*, and from the forthcoming Broadway musical

of the same name. I could hear the deafening applause as Sting finished his set and waited in the wings before he introduced me as the star of the show at Magicopolis. I know you're just dying to find out more about my gig with Sting, but I'm sorry, you'll have to wait. I want this first chapter to have a little suspense.

Sometimes (such as when Sting opens for me), I find it hard to believe that it was just

The author in his natural habitat.   over four decades ago that I was presenting magic tricks to open shows for the Eagles, Cheap Trick, the Spencer Davis Group, and other rock bands. In 1972, when eight-track tape players were the thing and before comedy clubs or open mic nights became popular nationwide, I was a senior at Taft High in Woodland Hills who practiced and polished his magic act as part of various showcases and talent contests all over Los Angeles. The experience was terrific. The money wasn't. These were all non-pay, on-the-job training type of gigs, and I felt fortunate to do them.

Clubs ran these shows on off nights and people could see me, along with folk singers, angry poets, and comics. On Monday nights I did the hootenanny at Doug Weston's Troubadour. On Tuesday nights I was at The Show Biz, owned by Murray, a guy who became famous for his appearances as the Unknown Comic on TV's *The Gong Show*. Wednesday at The Palomino, a cowboy hangout. I performed my magic tricks anywhere possible, for zero.

When I wasn't performing for free, it was my monotonous business to fold pants, and it was that drab drudgery that led to the creation of my Highdini act. I worked at the Tarzana branch of Pants Galore, a store that sold clothes that were rejects or severely flawed. We had bellbottoms where only one leg was flared, jeans with the back pockets sewn upside down, and belts with no holes for the buckle. The gimmick was that everything sold for five dollars.

In the store I developed a bunch of smart-ass answers to common questions. "Do your pants shrink?" "Only if you wash them." "How do your pants run?" "They don't." And so on.

Pants Galore was a small chain that did a lot of radio advertising. The commercials were the typical ordinary-type radio spots of the day, hard-sell boring assaults by a screaming announcer. "Blue jeans five dollars, Pants Galore...Corduroys five dollars, Pants Galore...Khakis five dollars, Pants Galore..." I hated those commercials, and so did everyone else.

The owner, I'll call him Barney because I think that was his name, was a nice guy who acted more like a buddy than a boss. One day he walked in just as one of his awful commercials was blasting at us from the radio. In a gentle sort of way I told him how dumb and boring I felt his advertising was. And suddenly I was given the opportunity to do something about it, to create my kind of commercial directed at my age group, who felt the same way I did and were the store's primary customers.

My brainchild was the Pants Galore Answer Man. Barney decided to try it. "Could you possibly record day after tomorrow?" I said, "I think I could work it in." The commercial included the same smart-ass answers to common questions I'd been using on the job. Now, not only was I the writer, but also I became the announcer. The commercial was recorded and aired on KWEST, the greatest rock radio station ever, and that's where I met Kyle Emorian.

Kyle sold radio advertising and his was the first hand I shook when I went to the station to record the spot. I showed Kyle some card tricks, and asked him to come see my act in a hippie coffeehouse at the Whole Earth Marketplace in the Encino neighborhood. He laughed and applauded louder than anyone. We became fast friends and Kyle started acting as my manager, which was fine with me.

Besides selling advertising to all the big rock clubs in town, Kyle also started selling me to these clubs as well. By the time I graduated high school in June of 1973 I was opening for bands like the Spencer Davis Group at The Whisky on the Sunset Strip and Cheap Trick at Starwood in West Hollywood.

At first it was extremely tough holding a rock club crowd's attention, but I learned how to make it work and audiences got off on me. Clubbers were watching, listening, and actually enjoying what I did. The process was slow but sure, and I felt myself improving each week, building my confidence as a rock magician.

I spent hour after hour, day after day, and month after month perfecting bits specifically suited to this niche audience, and my popularity continued to grow. That was cool. I made a ton of visits to Starwood and the Topanga Corral, among other clubs. I called myself "Highdini;" my act was inspired by Cheech & Chong, who had recently released their first comedy record album.

During the show, several big bouquets of marijuana appeared from nowhere then vanished in a puff of smoke. I snorted tablespoons of white powder, and as a finish to the bit I grabbed my nose and a long stream of salt-like stuff poured out. One by one eight smoking pipes magically appeared between my fingertips, which made me dry as a bone and "gave me cotton mouth," causing me to spit out dozens of cotton balls. It looked like I drank a huge thirst-quenching pitcher of beer in a fraction of an instant. I pretended to be a lit-tle stoned while I did these drug-inspired tricks, in the same way I assumed Dean Martin "acted" drunk when he sang songs.

Mastering these shows gave me a kind of power I had never felt before. At times I had total command of these crowds. I loved that these rock audiences were tough and I could actually entertain them. Every once in a while some-one would come up to me and ask "How did you do that?" or say "You're funny," and it would make my night. Of

William Brent

Highdini portrait that was reproduced on flyers, handbills, and DEA wanted posters.

course, they were always slurring their words, or on the verge of passing out, but that didn't matter. Meeting girls was also a nice little perk that came from performing.

At the Corral in Topanga Canyon I opened for The Flying Burrito Brothers, The Eagles, Neil Young & Crazy

Horse, and Little Feat, among other groups. Little Feat's Lowell George kept asking me if I could teach him how to cheat at gambling, which I couldn't.

For a couple years I was on the fringe of the LA rock club scene. My buddies treated me like a big shot, but I didn't experience any feeling of monetary accomplishment. I was just an unimportant act and my salary was small. Most rock clubs didn't budget for a magician, but I was a paid performer. I'd usually get $10 to $15 a show, which I guess in 1972 dollars wasn't that bad.

What was bad was that discos started to replace live entertainment in general and rock clubs in particular, and I was on the way to nowhere. Fortunately, I was still earning $1.65 per hour at Pants Galore; by working overtime, and with my employee discount, I was able to put together a fine wardrobe. I was particularly fond of standing in a pair of Earth shoes while wearing my paisley corduroy elephant bellbottoms with the humongous chrome square pirate belt buckle and the open tie-dyed double-knit shirt with turtleneck dickie and Nehru jacket ensemble.

It was the perfect outfit to wear with an embroidered blue jean top hat when Kyle booked Highdini on few and far between plum gigs: A charity benefit for the National Organization for the Reform of Marijuana Laws at the Playboy Mansion, a party thrown by Elton John on the back lot at Universal Studios, and an appearance at the National Fashion & Boutique Show in New York for Glass Head, a bong manufacturer.

Those appearances made me feel seven feet tall, but after a couple of big venue concert shows I felt like I could walk under a wiener dog while wearing that embroidered blue jean top hat. The first, opening for the aforementioned band Flash Cadillac and the Continental Kids, was a gig that may not have been one of the most humiliating moments of my life, but it came close, at the Colorado Springs Municipal Auditorium, which was packed beyond legal capacity.

Eight o'clock was the hour appointed for the beginning of the ordeal called The Flash Cadillac Pig Stomp & Surf Rodeo. As early as six o'clock, a crowd began to assemble outside the auditorium. At six-thirty, an attendant, by mistake, opened the doors. The fifteen hundred seats were immediately occupied. Approximately two hundred standees also fought their way inside. The show was the major big-deal event in Colorado Springs that night, and evidently every man, woman, child, cat, dog, and goat in town wanted to go.

Belatedly it was announced that only ticket holders would be permitted to attend the show. The police arrived and began to clear the room, to an accompaniment of cries of injustice, and here and there, slanderous references to the amorous activities with animals allegedly performed by some patrolman's mother. Once the herd was trimmed, those who waited nearly two hours for the show to begin were just as enraged as those who were forced to leave.

It was not a pleasant atmosphere, to say the least, especially for an unexpected opening act. When I was introduced, the rabid Flash fans' boos reached my ears. The next thing I knew, I was standing in a glare of light. The spotlight was so blinding that I saw nothing but black, except for the exit signs and a few red emergency lights. I couldn't see anyone, but the boos were getting louder. It was getting intense. I tried to cover the fact that my body was jolting, zapping, shaking . . . and continued to plow forward with my show.

I knew what I was doing wasn't working, so I changed my approach. My hands began to tremble, and my lips quivered. The unruly crowd booed so loud, I couldn't even hear myself speak. It felt like my throbbing heart was going to jump out of my chest, I was sweating profusely, and the floor felt like it was moving up and down. It was a disaster, and I was petrified.

Somehow, automatically I continued my routine, and, after some hesitation, I cut the act short. I did not bow my head in shame and slip out as might be expected of someone who had failed so miserably and publically. Instead, an automatic defense system seemed to kick in. That's when I gave the audience the finger with both hands, held my head high, and walked off with pride, to the blasting chorus of cold stares and heckles. I'm not really sure where that macho bravado came from, since my ego was definitely crushed. I felt as if I'd been run over by a truck.

So, when offered, I was hesitant to take last night's Sting gig, given that I was still somewhat pummeled by my most recent terrible rock audience rejection experience decades and decades ago. Just the thought of it gave me a flashback to my Flash Cadillac show. The strong sensation of the angry "booing" was more than a memory from forty years ago; it had left a footprint in my skull. I physically re-experienced the disaster that was.

Nevertheless, I'd agreed to this new assignment, mostly because of my wife, Bozena. She is a HUGE Sting fan who not only admires his poetic yoga meditative ways, but she also grew up in Poland listening to his music, yearning to one day attend one of his concerts, never dreaming she would actually get to meet him. I took this opportunity to make my wife happy. You know the old saying: "Happy wife, happy life." How could I refuse?

It all came together on November 4, 2013. An independent record label, Cherry Tree Records, engaged me, Sting, and Magicopolis, for an event designed to promote their newly signed unknown recording artists. Having Sting as the opener guaranteed an exclusive audience of everybody who was anybody when it comes to rock journalists and music insiders, who otherwise might not come out to hear the unknowns.

Sting was the draw, but the promoters also needed me. After Sting's set, the curtains closed and while his band equipment was switched for the other artist's gear, my job was to fill the time performing in front of the curtains. I, mostly unknown to the assembled guests, was there to keep the crowd engaged and amused so they wouldn't leave before the other widely unknowns took the stage.

I must do this. Tonight. Now. I had an attack of diarrhea. By the time I walked onto the stage, I did not have the confidence to do a stellar job. But I was in a thoroughly professional mood and did do a stellar job...the audience was in the palm of my hand. Nobody left or booed. I'm pleased to report that my comedy and magic was greeted with a roar of laughter and an outburst of cheering.

After the show Bozena and I were invited to share some time and be photographed with Sting. He charmed us when he said what a great theater we have, how he appreciated being able to actually see everyone's face in the audience from the stage, how he read that I had designed and built the venue myself.

With my backup singers, from left, Sting, and Bozena.

Bozena told him that in our full evening show she levitates to his song "Desert Rose." I chimed in with, "We heard you wrote and recorded it specifically for that purpose." Sting cracked a gracious smile and with great courtesy and kindness professed his fondness for magic, magicians, and all that is Magicopolis.

PART ONE

FIRST BEST JOBS

THE JOLLY JESTER

Aspen, at the top of the Rocky Mountains in Colorado, is an internationally famous ski resort and glitzy playground for the affluent. But in 1976 the Aspen vibe was not unlike the frat boy atmosphere depicted in the film *Animal House* and we would really come alive just after the moon came up. Everybody drank, did drugs, smoked, and made love, with no fear of addiction or disease or death. It seemed we all had permanent erections, hangovers, and everything was carefree and raucous and unplanned. In those days, we had all the fun we could each and every day.

I was twenty-one years old when I started a four-year tour of duty working for Bob Sheets as a magician/bartender at The Jolly Jester. My fancy salary was thirty dollars before taxes per eight-hour shift plus tips. That was, of course, just a starting salary. In slightly over three years my superior talents were recognized and I was upped to thirty-five dollars before taxes per eight-hour shift plus tips. Actually I exaggerated about the eight-hour part, as it was usually longer. The shift started around 4:00 p.m., après-ski time, and went all night to the first hours of the morning till I was unconscious, subconscious, nauseous, or all three.

Bob has always been smart, talented, and inspiring, with a round face, thick neck, twinkly eyes, big moustache, and gap-toothed smile. Mr. Sheets has a sense of the whimsy, a sense of the absurd, and when his imagination takes off and he gets to the child part of himself, he giggles and carries on like a little kid. That's how he became known as the Jolly Jester—hence the bar's name. In 1975, Bob had been hired as a bartender just outside Aspen, in Snowmass, at country-pop singer John Denver's Tower Restaurant.

Sheets quickly became a successful local legend behind the bar, mixing drinks and merriment with his comedy and magic. So much so, that the following winter a patron sponsored Bob and he opened his own bar in Aspen. He knew he couldn't do it alone—eight hours a day, seven days a week, was too much time for one magician to fill, no matter how talented they were, and would only lead to burnout. As it turned out, we both burned out. But it was a wild ride for the handful of tourist seasons that it lasted.

Bob was a consummate professional who became a valued lifelong friend, and I learned more from him, and the job he gave me, than I realized at the time. One of the great educational benefits from the work was a practical understanding of the art and science of audience management. People who are oiling their throats with alcohol are generally not shy when they see how a trick is done, and it's a great help to know where corrections are needed. Most of the bar-hopping crowd changed five times a night, which enabled me to perfect tricks by doing them over and over and over, forty or fifty times a week. By trial and error my sleight of hand, timing, presentation, and other elements improved.

I absorbed much of what I know about comedy from the bar crowd. I learned to not work too hard at being funny, not to imitate myself from the night before, to try to make each performance as if it were the first time I'd ever done it, how to improvise, how to take advantage of a situation with a quick ad lib—like when a guy was at the bar for several hours, drinking continuously, hurling shot after shot against his tonsils, and then, without a word, would fall over backwards onto the floor, out cold. I might say something like "I like a man who knows when to stop."

Bob also trained me as a bartender and taught me how to use magic to sell more cocktails. "The more you drink, the better the tricks look." One key strategy that I learned is to never perform a trick until all the drinks are half full. That way, when the trick is over, everyone is ready for a new round. Patrons were unconsciously trained—now it's time to watch a trick, now it's time to buy a drink—and Pavlov would have loved it. "Don't applaud, keep on drinking," was a motto I learned quickly.

Bob was, and is, also an amazing street magician. In the early days, Bob stood in front of The Jester and performed his street act. Instead of passing the hat, he pied pipered folks into the bar. Once inside, Bob introduced me. I sold drinks and did tricks, while Bob went outside and gathered another group. In an hour, a big crowd pressed around the bar. Word got around, and after a few days Bob no longer needed to work the street; from then on things just exploded.

Bob Sheets and me at The Jester, dressed like real men.

The bar was long; that shelf could support at least thirty pairs of elbows. Four feet behind the bar were long benches to sit on with a ledge that ran atop the benches that was just wide enough, if you were young and a little athletic, to stand on. People were sitting at the bar, standing on the floor, sitting on the benches, and standing on top of the benches from one end to the other. And the crowd was wired. Crazed. Insane.

The lights were low, the rock and roll was loud, and we would announce "We're about to do some magic and there'll be no drinks for ten minutes, so get 'em now." To serve everyone would take twenty to thirty minutes. Nobody ever died of thirst at The Jester; even competent drinkers were overserved, and mixing the drinks was a big part of the show.

"Want a lime in that gin & tonic?" I pretended to take a lime out of the wastebasket, washed it off, and dropped it in the drink. "Don't worry, the alcohol will kill any germs." When someone ordered a beer we didn't have, such as Moosehead Ale, Bob responded, "No problemo." He opened and poured a bottle of Budweiser, and then, with a felt tip pen, crossed out the word "Bud" and wrote "Moosehead." "One Moosehead, drink up," he'd say.

We did a substantial business serving upside down margaritas—no glass necessary. Customers laid their heads on the bar, mouths open. With a bottle of Triple Sec in one hand and Roses's Lime in the other, I poured, and then I quickly switched the two bottles for sweet & sour and tequila, completing the task until mouths were overflowing. Customers just had to sit up and swallow.

Regulars brought friends in from far and wide for our margaritas. If they winked and tipped in advance, the newcomer would get a special upside down margarita. When they sat up their face was met with a cream pie. Actually, it was a coffee filter filled with whipped cream.

"This is the craziest bar in town," said one smartly dressed young man to his equally decked-out friend. They ordered Heineken drafts and the first guy secretly let me know his buddy was a first-time visitor. Just as the beers were served, I pretended to accidentally knock one over. The stranger jumped to his feet to avoid ruining his clothes while his friend burst into uproarious laughter. The knocked-over glass was a fakeroo with solid contents, a means of initiating newcomers to the fun at The Jester.

The gag over, I removed the fake glass and served real beer. The instigator didn't notice the switch. "Look, it's a fake beer," so saying, he grabbed the newly served glass and threw the contents into his friend's face.

Suddenly the music stopped, the lights went up to last-call brightness, and the magic show was on. Bob and I would do a total of about ten minutes of our best stuff, the crowd would cheer, the lights would go down, the rock music cranked up, and we'd be back serving drinks. That's how it went from late afternoon until the early morning hours night after night after night. Sometimes we locked the doors and kept going beyond the legal hours and I went home in daylight.

Customers were just as wild, raw, and often more spontaneous and ridiculous than we were. In the winter knit beanies and ski caps were popular and I had a trick where I asked to borrow one. A girl put her lacy red bra on the bar, "will this work?" and then she kindly showed everyone where it came from—her chest. The crowd cheered, and she made several new friends.

One summer we had a bowl of goldfish sitting on the back bar. Now and then, we apparently grabbed a live one outta the water, popped it in our mouth, and chewed it up. In reality, we just pretended to eat the live sushi. Actually, a secret switch was made and we ate carrots cut to an approximate goldfish shape. It was a great trick.

People started to hear about the goldfish-eating and wanted to see it done. A regular customer brought in a younger brother on holiday from college. The brother was impressed with the fish stunt, and I let him in on the carrot secret. I told him, "In the next hour we're going to ask for volunteers. Raise your hand and I'll put a carrot in your mouth—you'll be a hero." When the time came, I put a real live wiggling goldfish in his mouth. The carrot was the bait, and the college kid was the fish that was filleted; everyone cried laughing.

One night I opened the bar and the first person through the door was an attractive young girl. She asked, "Are you into yoga?" In a fraction of an instant she was on the floor going through various contortions. I excused this rather bizarre behavior as part of the phenomenon of people saying strange things and behaving even more strangely at The Jester. "Why don't you get up on the bar so we can get a better look at what you're doing?" She swiftly stripped down to a sheer leotard and happily knotted her legs behind her head, intertwined with mangled arms, both legs straight up on either side of her head. Thereafter she visited The Jester every couple weeks. Her many bar-top performances never failed to be crowd-pleasing events.

A number of well-known names of the time got into the spirit of the place and surprised us, including Buddy Hackett, Ted Kennedy, Cheech & Chong, Jimmy Buffet, Hunter Thompson, and Farrah Fawcett. In those days, before cell phone cameras, tabloid TV, and the Internet, Bob and I often witnessed the questionable, inappropriate, and embarrassing antics of captains of industry, movie actors, and sports stars.

The Jester environment ran the gamut from innovative magic to spontaneous outrageous comedy, an irreplaceable training ground I was privileged to be a part of. The principal thing I learned at The Jester NOT to do with my life was to be perpetually plastered, wasted, loaded, and stoned. Those days are long over for me. A quick word to my younger readers: in the long run, there are three types of people who can't handle constant drugging, drinking, and smoking—magicians, comedians, and everybody else.

THE LEMON TRICK

Bob and I each became known at The Jester for particular feats of magic we performed individually. Those particular tricks became signature bits, because our regulars were hardy souls who seemed to have no purpose in life except to bring in newbies and request that we show them their favorite mysteries. Tourists paid the bills and locals helped promote us to them. I was best known for my rendition of The Lemon Trick. I did not originate the idea, but I did re-envision the effect—the trick as perceived by the audience, the method, the secrets and details that make the effect effective, and how the effect and method are presented.

It was back in 1969, when I was almost fifteen years old and got hired to do a show for a bunch of Cub Scouts (which put me on a search for tricks that would pack small, play big, and cost little or nothing), that I was first introduced to The Lemon Trick. It was Dai Vernon, one of my mentors you'll be reading about later in this book, who told me about a vaudeville sleight of hand magician, Emil Jarrow, and The Lemon Trick. I started fooling with this bit back then, developing various methods and routines, but it wasn't until I had the opportunity at The Jester to workshop the trick dozens of different ways for dozens of different audiences weekly, that it gelled into a funny, elegant hit with audiences. But I'm getting ahead of myself.

Some new tricks fall into place rather quickly for me when I test them. Some are tried and discarded easily, based on audience reaction, others, like this one, can take years to simplify and routine into a thing of beauty. After Vernon described how The Lemon Trick looked, he didn't tell me how it was done. The Professor gave hints, but no directions.

He said, "You're a very clever boy. It'll be good for you to figure it out. You'll come up with something; just don't stop thinking too soon." It was a challenge I was happy to accept.

By 1969, I'd been a student of magic for several months shy of a decade and was a fixture at the Magic Castle, a private club for magicians, for a few years. I had become absolutely obsessed with the craft and had seen each and every magician at the Magic Castle perform numerous times, literally dozens of guys. Not ONE of them did The Lemon Trick. So I never saw a properly performed example of how it might look in person.

Nor could I find it in the definitive original five-volume encyclopedic authority on magic tricks, *Tarbell Course in Magic.* I found the section on tricks with paper money, which included Scarne's Bill Change, Grant's Slow Motion Bill Transposition, LePaul's Torn Bill, Topsy-Turvy Bill…but there was no sign of Jarrow's Bill in Lemon Trick.

How could this trick be such a winner in the 1920s and it was not even mentioned anywhere in Tarbell? And out of all the dozens of great magicians at the Castle, I hadn't seen or heard of even one guy doing it since the place opened in 1963? The reason was, at least partly, that Jarrow never published a how-to guide for his peers, and apparently never taught or authorized his invention for use by anyone; although there's irrefutable evidence that unauthorized copycats existed in his day. How I happened to develop my particular Lemon Trick formula—and "happened" is the proper word since the evolution of the routine, like a good many in my repertoire, was not purely a matter of calculation, but a case of extensive trial and error—will require that we go back to the description of the trick Vernon gave me in 1969:

"Jarrow borrowed three bills, paper money of any denomination, which were tightly rolled together into the shape of a fat cigarette, wrapped it in a handkerchief, and the bundle was held by a volunteer. A lemon was placed under a drinking glass. Jarrow pulled the handkerchief out of the guy's hands, and the cash was gone. The lemon was cut in half, and stuck in one of the halves were the rolled-up borrowed bills."

The Professor went on to tell me that the trick was Jarrow's closer; he became famous for it, and it helped make

him a vaudeville star. "During the early twenties when a theater marquee advertised the then-new stage illusion, Sawing
A Woman in Half, which was at the peak of its popularity,
the marquee across the street, where Jarrow was appearing,
advertised his act as Sawing a Lemon In Half."

Often when magicians do a torn and restored trick with a
playing card or a newspaper or a dollar bill for that matter,
one torn piece is kept by a spectator, so that when the rest
of the destroyed paper is magically restored, there is one
piece missing, and the retained one is shown to fit in like a
puzzle piece, "proving" the restored paper is the originally
destroyed one. When a magician makes a playing card vanish and reappear in his pocket or an envelope or his wallet,
often the card is signed by a volunteer, also as a proof, for
the same identification reasons. So I asked The Professor if
Jarrow used either of those methods of identification to verify in the audience's mind that the vanished three bills were
the same ones that appeared in the lemon?

He said no torn corners, no signatures, no written serial
numbers, but that one identifying factor was the combination of bills borrowed was always different. One time it
might be three fives, or a ten and two singles, or a twenty,
a ten and a two dollar bill. The Roaring Twenties were a
sustained period of economic prosperity—in addition to the
currency we have today, there were also five hundred-, one
thousand-, five thousand-, and even ten thousand- dollar
bills in circulation. On top of that, Vernon said that people
always recognized their money. What? Of course, when I
presented my teenage version of the trick as described, none
of my crowd was positively convinced that the vanished bills
were the same ones that appeared in the lemon. It seemed
odd that wasn't the case in Jarrow's time . . .

Until I discovered that 1910's American paper money was
25% bigger than 1920's money, and 1920's money was 25%
larger than today's currency. The bills Jarrow borrowed for
the trick were up to 50% larger than today, making it an easy
matter to recognize blemishes, such as, for instance, a coffee

stain on a president's face, and low-digit serial numbers on the various denominations were a quarter to a half-inch tall in the 1910s and 20s. The kind of paper money in circulation before July of 1929, when the Treasury Department began the distribution of the small bills we know today, was just plain HUGE.

Along the road to my development of an interpretation of Jarrow's trick, I made a few key decisions. My first decision was to positively authenticate the magical transposition of just *one* bill. I felt that in the audience's mind that would enhance the mystery, simplify the presentation, strengthen the effect, and negate any purpose in borrowing three bills.

As I mentioned, there could be various methods of authentication. Someone could write down the serial number of the bill before it vanished, a torn corner could be held by a helper and after the vanished money appeared in the lemon the torn corner could be matched to the bill, or someone could autograph or initial their name on the cash before it transposed from one place to another.

Yet there are inherent problems with these methods. Though the great thing about the torn corner idea is that it's very visual, and everyone gets it as a convincer right away, the issue is that a minute later, the smart ones realize the possibility that the tiny corner could have been easily switched for one torn from a bill previously put in the lemon. The serial number idea doesn't even have the instantaneous visual like the corner, and it's no secret that stacks of consecutive serial numbered bills are available at any bank— erase the last digit and you have the same duplicate bill solution like the torn corner. Again, it's too easy for the smart ones to figure out. The autograph has the instant visual of the corner, negates the idea of a switch or duplicate bill; hence, as far as I'm concerned, it is and always will be a crucial factor in maximizing this mystery.

So the decision was made to use one signed bill. The next issue to conquer was the timing. The best effect you can get with a magical transposition—that's the category The

Lemon Trick falls into—is when the time between seeing the thing in one place, and then another, is reduced to instantaneous. If a person vanishes on stage, than a fraction of an instant later appears in the audience, the effect is amazing. For the same trick, if the person disappears and ten minutes later is spotted in the crowd, it might be great, but it wouldn't qualify as amazing.

Maybe audiences way back when were less demanding and more easily impressed—who knows? When I vanished the money from under a handkerchief, the time lapse was too long between actually seeing the borrowed money and its reappearance in the lemon. After even a few seconds, many were thinking and some even wondered out loud, "Hey, is the money still in the handkerchief or are they holding a wad of nothing?"

It was an easy task to put the cash in an envelope and burn it before it appeared in the lemon and make the sequence a laugh riot with clever comments, but as far as heightening the mystery, there was the same time lapse problem. Ideally one needed to see the autographed currency vanish and in a fraction of an instant see the very same signed-money appear in the lemon. My solution was an at-the-fingertips barehanded disappearance of the cash.

So I figured that out—they'd see the bill disappear, instantly the lemon was cut in half, and stuck in one of the halves was the tightly rolled up borrowed money. Not too bad—or so it seemed. But it was not too good either. Audiences were impressed, and all went well, except that only a few seconds after the trick, people were saying, "...Was the bill really in the lemon? Is the money wet? Does the cash smell like lemon?"

Convincing proof needed to be embedded in the audience's mind that the money was really inside the lemon. So I kept the style of vanishing the money, and its instantaneous reappearance in the lemon to create the magic moment, but I did it in a way so that spectators were certain a moment later that the bill really had appeared at the center of that juicy fruit.

Instead of the instant image of half a lemon with a rolled-up bill snatched from it, my solution, when the lemon was cut, was that only a speck of green was visible. The knife was used to dig the bill out of the lemon, selling the fact that it was really embedded in the meat of the fruit.

But there were still a number of other bits of polish to make this a winner. As a magician who stood behind a bar making drinks between doing tricks, there were a lot of distractions in our rowdy saloon that could take away your audience's focus.

What helped to capture a crowd of eighty to ninety drinkers, and riveted their attention on a small trick with a lemon, were a few strategically placed human anchors. Instead of one volunteer loaning and signing the money, I engaged other helpers at either end as well as in the middle of the bar, widening the focus of the trick into more of a production. Vernon was the man who taught me that most magicians stop thinking about a trick too soon, and I never wanted to be lumped into that group. Here's how the finished product looked:

A bowl of lemons sat on top of the cash register with a little sign that said "Lemon Trick." When people wondered what that bowl of lemons with the little sign was all about, I was happy to show them if they were kind enough to loan some money.

"...A twenty, fifty, or one hundred dollar bill works best. Okay! Let's give John D. Rockefeller a big applause for coming up with the hundred bucks." As the crowd gave John the clap, I tossed his hundred dollar bill into the tip jar and said... "For my next trick..." everyone laughed, I retrieved the bill, "...just kidding, we'll go ahead and do the trick with this five John gave me..." It really was John's hundred, my comment was just another joke.

With a felt tip pen I drew on the money, "The first thing we do is put the glasses on Franklin so that he watches the trick as carefully as you folks do. One of the few federal offenses you'll see here." I pointed to a pretty girl seated in the middle of the bar, "Who are you, what's your name? Good to meet you. Please take the pen, and on the front, the back, or if you're really clever, on the edge of the bill, write your name. Thank you, oh isn't that nice, she also wrote her phone number . . . and it's an 800 number."

I walked the length of the bar pointing out her signature, then folded the bill four times so that it became a small packet with her autograph still visible. Folding instead of rolling, so the signature was still visible, was a tiny detail that enhanced the trick start to finish, because those close to the action noticed the name both when the money disappeared and instantly when it later reappeared in the lemon, virtually impossible to arrange if the bill were rolled up.

The hundred was clipped into a doctor's hemostatic clamp—the type that look like scissors and are commonly used by pot smokers—and handed to a man at one end of the bar. "You get to be the barbeque tongs monitor . . . actually that's a vital surgical tool—roach clips. Hold it up high so everyone can keep an eye on the money with her name."

The clips were a nice way to display the bill until it was needed, but I started using them because after the trick, occasionally intelligent onlookers said the bill in the lemon might have been switched by tricky fingers for the signed one upon its removal. That's not the secret, but also not a bad guess. Using the clips to remove the bill at the trick's finish negated that speculation.

At the other end of the bar I handed a big steak knife to a guy, "You get to be the knife monitor—you look like you might be familiar with knives. Hold it high, about even with the roach clips. I hope you like the trick. You look a lot like Charlie Manson . . ."

Next, I returned to the center of the bar and displaying a small purple cloth bag with gold drawstrings—the type that surrounded new bottles of the Crown Royal whisky we served—reached into the bag and took out a piece of fruit. "In this ratty old bag is the mystery orange, which today is a lemon—that's the mystery." After showing the lemon, it was returned to the bag, and the girl who autographed the hundred was instructed to hold the bag up high, even with the roach clips and the knife.

I looked up and down the bar at the three helpers holding the stuff, "Makes kind of a nice picture, don't cha think? Okay, we better go ahead and do the trick. This is a very quick trick...it's like a snake bite when it happens. So don't cough or blink or look away, or you'll miss it."

The bill was taken from the clips. I told the guy to keep the clips handy, since they would be needed in just a second, and walked down the bar so everyone got a clear look at the girl's signature on the hundred. I stopped in front of her and asked, "Is your name still on the bill?" If everyone couldn't clearly hear "Yes," I had her say it again louder. It was not only an important presentational point before the money vanished, but also a dress rehearsal for her all-important "Yes" at the trick's finish.

"Okay, everyone ready? It's at the fingertips..." I wiggled my fingers, "Yes he will, no he won't," and as the money vanished into thin air I said, "Now you see it, now you don't...Quick, who has the lemon?" The girl screamed, "I've got it," as did the man when I asked, "Who has the knife?" The lemon was cut in two, and for a fraction of an instant it looked like something went wrong and that I tried to cover it up with some jokes.

"If the trick worked...inside the lemon...uh, well...lemon juice...Does anyone have another hundred? I know I can do it...Wait just a second...Can you see it? Can you see it in there?" I pointed out a speck of green in the center of the lemon. Using the knife, the bill was excavated so it stuck halfway out. As I walked the halved lemon with the bill stuck in it over to the guy with the roach clips, I could hear a few "no ways," "wows," and audible gasps.

"Using the roach clips, reach inside, so everyone can see that bill come out of the fruit..." As the bill emerged the rest of the way out I hollered, "It's a boy!" I grabbed the clips holding the cash, walked them to the center of the bar, and had the girl who signed remove the money from the clips. "Unfold that bill very carefully. I'll ask you one question—please answer in a loud clear voice, yes or no, do you see your name on that hundred-dollar bill?"

"Yes, oh yes, YES!" The crowd roared. I told her, "You were a great help, you can go ahead and keep the hundred!" Another joke. In fact, when the hundred was returned to its rightful owner, nearly every single solitary time, it was donated to the tip jar. Perhaps some of the reasons—the money was integrated into the trick, the mystery and humor had people laughing and wanting to give—but it is likely that part of the tip givers' generosity could be attributed to the fact that no one wants to put wet sticky money in their wallet. The Lemon Trick is, intrinsically, the most perfect magic trick that anyone working for tips could ever do—past, present, or in eternity.

Near the end of the Jester years, a friend who was also a bartending magician asked that I teach him my Lemon Trick routine. Being unusually charitable about the matter, I did so, and it has subsequently been a source of profound regret that I did.

Down the road I got a call from this friend, who I had generously taught for free and who had been making behind-the-bar tips from my gift. He called to tell me that he had taught my routine on an instructional videotape that would be sold to magicians worldwide.

If he were to tell the truth, I think he would have to agree that he wasn't exactly calling to ask for my permission since the tape had already been made. In fact, he wasn't even offering me any compensation. Plus his call was so late in coming that it was obvious he was just attempting to soften the surprise that the video would be released the following week.

When I demanded to know what he felt gave him the right to sell my routine, his answer was "It's a cornerstone of my bar show, I've been doing it a long time." I asked, "If you sang a Beatles song in your bar show would that entitle you to sell licenses to others to sing that song?" Apparently he could not comprehend the analogy or logic or refused to understand what I was trying to say. "Don't worry Steve, I gave you complete credit, your name is all over it, it's advertised right on the box as Steve Spill's Lemon Trick!" As if to prove what an ethical guy he was, he claimed, he "almost" called me the night of the filming. But he didn't.

I felt betrayed, rooked, cheated, victimized, violated, and should have screamed at the top of my lungs, "Hey, that routine doesn't belong to you to sell, and you know it, and you have no right to do it, cease and desist!" But I'm ashamed to say I didn't blast him with blazing guns like I would have now.

When I hung up, something odd happened. I immediately started feeling guilty that maybe it was my own fault, mine entirely for teaching him in the first place. I started beating myself up about putting so much temptation in the man's way and forcing him to selfishly exploit my work and gift on videotape for his own private gain. It seems to me now, in a long backward glance, absolutely crazy to have blamed myself instead of putting the blame on him where it belonged. I had been robbed.

Other pros in my circle knew the facts, but even today, in an era when music downloaders are prosecuted for theft, ASCAP collects royalty fees from stores that play background music, and emails receive automatic copyright protection, when it comes to the craft of magic, original expressions are generally not afforded copyrights, trademarks, or patents. And thus, there was nothing to be gained by driving myself crazy about this situation.

In fact, newer generations have also produced and sold nearly word-for-word, move-for-move instructional versions of my routine—some with only the very slightest of subtle variations, however trivial they may be, like different jokes, and some not even knowing they're doing my thing.

Today, the fact remains that I have seen and heard of similar frustrating situations between magicians going as far back as my memory goes, long before I started developing my Lemon Trick routine. When it comes to resolving episodes like these, there are exceptions to every rule of course.

But in our tiny magic world, only very rarely does a confrontation, attempt at a legal remedy, or a threat of bodily harm result in anything more than aggravation of the person who has right on their side. As you might expect, it's usually better to put your energy elsewhere, like writing about it in a book. They say that Jesus had always forgiven, even when nailed to the cross. But Jesus never developed an original routine for, or resurrected, the long dead Lemon Trick.

BUSKING

Making magic at the bar in Aspen was seasonal work. Sure, we had local patrons, but its survival was tourist dependent. Winter and summer we had tourists, but when spring sprung and fall fell The Jester would close for six to eight weeks during the off seasons.

I spent spring 1976 on a coast-to-coast busking tour with my friend Johnny Fox. Busking is thought of as a fancy word for street performing, but by definition, it also includes indoor hat passing. We traveled in Fox's vintage auto, which was in constant need of repair. We often ran out of gas and had flat tires. All the ailments known to vehicles depending upon internal combustion afflicted that jalopy. Often we'd be barreling along the highway in this barely roadworthy hunk-a-junk, one of us trying to steer with one hand while playing with a deck of cards or a coin in the other. Today Johnny drives fine late model rides with two hands firmly on the wheel, and he is a successful sword swallower on Ye Olde Renaissance Pleasure Faire circuit.

In 1976, though, he wasn't yet dressing like Robin Hood and spewing the words, "Young sire, can thoust please add thy email to my list?" Fox was, however, a talented sleight of hander specializing in coin tricks, who liked performing outdoors in the daytime. I specialized in sleight of hand with playing cards and preferred performing indoors in the evening. We played with cards and coins morning, noon, and night. Usually I fell asleep with a deck of cards in my hands.

We never spent more than a few days anywhere. It was tonight and then tomorrow would be today again. New day, new locale, and we never got tired of it. We had no other cares or interests besides busking, and our lives were scheduled around it. Most people were extraordinarily generous. Almost everywhere we stopped to do a show someone offered us a place to stay, food, drinks, money—they knew we didn't have much money, but it wasn't because they thought we were poor that they were so kind, but rather because they enjoyed our tricks, and above all, because they wanted to offer tokens of friendship to traveling strangers.

The South seemed to work best for us—Austin, New Orleans, Memphis, Key West—these were some of the cities where we found success. But we worked everywhere. We did our magic commando style—with no introduction, no permission, just right into the routine. I walked into a crowded bar, often connected to a restaurant with a long dinner wait, or a tavern full of construction workers, or a disco, and I went right up to a table, or the bar, and interrupted conversation with a fan of cards. "Reach in and grab one," I'd insist.

If someone grabbed a card, I was on my way. "Show everyone your card, I won't look, I've seen the trick before," I ordered. The selected card disappeared, floated, or changed to another card. Sometimes they just kept the card, said "Thanks," then put it in their pocket and walked away, or tore it up, or I'd get kicked out of places by restaurant managers or bartenders, but I didn't care, I just went somewhere else.

If I was able to complete that first trick and got a decent response, I continued for five or ten minutes and then held out my hat and said, "Help me get a room tonight." When I'd successfully entertained a little group of folks, others in the vicinity would notice and want to have fun too.

One time a restaurant manager in Atlanta watched me pass the hat. "Hey, you can't panhandle in here," he warned. "It's offensive to our guests. Now get outta here!" The six people I was amusing left with us and took Johnny and me out to dinner elsewhere.

Once we learned the hard way, though, about going into business with fellow buskers who we didn't know as well. We were at a Phoenix coffee shop, and it was there that we spotted Fernando. He ripped a page from his sketchpad and walked the paper over to a table where an elderly woman was seated. Hardly a word passed between the two, the woman took the paper, smiled, and handed him five dollars. Fernando returned to his table and started busily drawing in his sketchpad. After about five minutes, he walked up to Fox and handed him a piece of paper; on it was a perfectly rendered pencil sketch of Fox.

We hit it off right away, and Fernando temporarily joined our tour. Our Latin brother was one of us—a clever busker. He didn't spend a lot of energy gathering a crowd, doing a show, or passing a hat. He leisurely drew pictures and let his talent do the talking.

Little did we know that Fernando was a Mexican citizen who felt his talent also made him a US citizen. America felt differently. The last time that the three of us were on tour together, we were between Arizona and Texas when we were stopped at an immigration checkpoint. The officers asked for our identification, and Fox and I complied, but Fernando did not. They detained him and informed us he would be deported. We were fingerprinted, photographed, and accused of smuggling an illegal alien.

We tried to explain that it had all been a simple misunderstanding and that we didn't know Fernando's citizenship status. But under a strict interpretation of the law we were guilty. They let us off with a stern warning. "If we catch you harboring or aiding and abetting a fugitive again, you'll be convicted of smuggling an illegal alien, charged a hefty fine, and lose your citizenship...plus we'll toss you in jail and throw away the key." As I remember it, not only was he embarrassed, but Fox was also so upset he threw away the beautifully rendered pencil portrait Fernando had sketched of him. He never wanted to be reminded of our criminal behavior.

It took a while for Fox to locate a good spot in San Antonio, Texas. He started working his magic at the edge of a park, at the bottom of a hill, near a busy intersection. Today, when Johnny does his sword-swallowing act he can entertain hundreds at a time. In 1976, Fox was a coin man who was a master at entertaining an up close group of ten people.

While Johnny was in the park making silver dollars appear and disappear at his fingertips, I was scouting out The Riverwalk in San Antonio, looking for bars to return to that evening, bars where people might appreciate sophisticated, properly performed card tricks. I picked my spots, and went to meet up with Fox, who was working his magic at the edge of a park. As I walked down the hill toward the park, I saw a huge crowd, maybe a hundred people. As I got closer, I saw Fox making four silver dollars appear. Then, one at a time, the coins became invisible, a routine I'd seen him do a million times. I couldn't believe the size of the crowd he'd drawn. Johnny had finally done it; the hat was gonna be huge on this one.

As I got even closer, I saw that about ten people were engaged in Fox's routine. The other ninety people were looking behind Fox, across the street, at a man standing on the roof of a ten-story building. It looked like he was gonna jump. Was he really gonna do it?

Everything seemed to happen in slow motion. It was dead quiet as we watched the figure high above, dive head first, straight down. Spectators blocked my view of the landing, but I can tell you the accelerated speed of his departure from the roof to his meeting with the surface of the sidewalk produced a loud, sickening, thud. I half heard it, half felt the impact come through the earth—and I was across the street. It was a haunting memory.

I learned something very valuable that day. The juxtaposition between whatever devastating agony that might drive a man to suicide and the simple little surprises and merriment Fox dispensed made me realize what an important service we magicians offer. People need fun like they need food and water and sleep. Even if it's only for a brief period of time, guys like Johnny and I can relieve the pain or boredom of everyday life. When audiences experience our magic, it's a sign that maybe the future will hold even more fun. Fun isn't just fun—it's hope.

WHEN BOB WAS BESS AND I WAS HARRY

It was built in 1920 as a private school for girls. It was Jack Davis's Brook Farm restaurant in the thirties, then a tearoom, a country inn, a French restaurant, and another French restaurant. Between the two French restaurants, circa 1980–1985, it was the Brook Farm Inn of Magic, home of a two-man dinner theater show, starring me, and master funny tricky person, Bob Sheets.

The barn-looking building was nestled in a residential country-like setting in the Washington DC suburb of Chevy Chase, Maryland. Inside was a large rustic pine paneled room with a stone fireplace, beamed ceiling, and deer head trophies. We kept the decor just the way it had been for the last fifty years or so, adding only a stage, curtains, and some theatrical lights.

The show was a mix of classic tricks, illusions, and magic parodies that we called *Magicomedy Cabaret*. It ran for five years, 290 times a year, a total of 1,450 performances, 2,175 hours on stage. Due to circumstances beyond our control, not every show was perfect. Murphy's Law—everything that can go wrong will go wrong, acquired an addendum...and everything that can't possibly go wrong will also go wrong, especially with our levitation routine.

The cast of *Magicomedy Cabaret*, me and Bob Sheets.

Normally, the floating lady volunteer from the audience looked like this: After a lengthy dissertation about the profound achievement the audience was about to witness and a ridiculous volunteer selection process, followed by a long and flamboyant hypnosis procedure, our woman of choice took off her shoes and reclined on a plywood board supported by two sawhorses. Then the female, and the board below her, slowly rose into the air above the sawhorses.

A hula-hoop was passed around our floater to prove she was really floating and not connected to anything. More mystical gestures, and our girl and board returned to the sawhorses. The hypnotic trance was broken and the volunteer safely returned to the audience.

Bozena is lighter than air at Magicopolis.

One time, after our usual dramatic comedy introduction, selection process, hypnotizing, and magical mystical gestures, the giggly party girl refused to levitate. She just lay there—ten minutes of comedy build-up and no payoff. We felt like jerks.

Another time, a pretty young woman was happily floating in midair, but Bob and I couldn't seem to summon the power to return her to Earth. Bob threw her over his shoulder and carried her to safety—in the air above the sawhorses was the levitating plywood board. I passed the hula-hoop around the board to prove it was really floating with nothing supporting it.

Third time's the charm. The exquisite woman lying on our plywood board looked like the queen of Sheba. She was so international, and so glamorous, in her low-cut evening gown. As the board started to go up, her right breast started to go out. I passed the hoop around her boob to prove there was nothing supporting it.

Yet another time, our floating volunteer couldn't stop laughing and sneezing. She laughed and sneezed so hard that she started peeing and couldn't stop. Her laughing and sneezing and peeing soaked and rocked the floating board she was lying on so violently that she nearly fell off. The audience was rolling in the aisles.

In another of our favorite tricks I was Harry Houdini, and Bob, in drag, played my wife Bess Houdini with our rendition of the classic *Metamorphosis*. A committee of volunteers from the audience critically examined a wooden packing crate in which I was locked. Under the watchful eyes of the committee Bob vanished and I immediately appeared in his place. The box was opened and therein was found Mrs. Houdini.

On one such occasion, Houdini had a large Mexican lunch and was locked in the crate with lots of trapped gas. At the moment Bob was ready to vanish and I was to reappear in his place, the most prolonged and mighty scented wind of methane ever escaped from me. Startled for a fraction of an instant, I lost my footing during the switcheroo with Bob and sharply twisted my ankle, which cracked like an egg. The adrenaline really flowed and I was caught up in the action. With pain shooting through my ankle, I knew I was hurt. How badly I was hurt remained to be seen. Like a crusty old football player, I figured I'd bounce back and told myself I was fine. Staggering to my feet, I finished the trick and the show as if nothing was wrong.

At that moment, Bob was trapped in the crate with my backdoor breeze and the odor was overwhelming. Tears welled up in his eyes. The volunteers removing the chains and locks were a little slow. When the crate was finally unlocked and we were about to release Bob, I screamed, "We gotta get him out quick, when I was in the box I broke wind." The line worked great and I kept it in the act.

That night I took a load of Excedrin PMs. I don't know how I ever managed to sleep that night, but I must have dozed, because I knew the instant I was awake, the pain began again, and I knew, without any hesitation, something was royally messed up. You've heard the old theater saying, "Break a leg?" That's what I'd done, but in this case it was my ankle. I was in excruciating pain and my ankle was the size of a grapefruit. Had I not had a frame of steel and an abnormal will to live, I might have died of the injury. Okay, that's not true, it actually was more painful of a fracture than severe. Otherwise I was as good as new. The ankle was put in a plaster cast and with the aid of a cane I could still do the show, except for the Houdini routine, which was physically too demanding.

A member of our illustrious staff was rehearsed to take my place in the Houdini bit.

The routine took on a new dimension of humor since my stand-in didn't speak. He wasn't a mute, just a little shy in front of 150 people. We had a solution. He wore the Houdini outfit and did the trick, but I did the dialogue with Bob.

One funny sequence happened when Bob slammed the lid on the box and it looked like my stand-in's hand was smashed. His hand was smashed and I'm the one who screamed in pain. Bob lifted the lid and I showed everyone—actually, my stand-in showed everyone—it was just a fake rubber hand. Bob and I capped the bit by singing a few bars of the Village People's "Macho, Macho Man."

The situation brought a lot of new comedy to the routine. Bob and I felt pretty comfortable with this new arrangement. Then the show came when the stand-in's hand really did get smashed. He had fractured fingers, I had a broken ankle, and the Houdini bit went on hiatus for six weeks.

Between the illusions (that's what we magic types call the tricks with larger props like people or big boxes), Bob and I alternated doing standup routines. My version of the aged Magic Coloring Book trick was a favorite. It started with a story about my boyhood visits to the barbershop. While getting my haircut I developed a taste for beautiful women by looking at *Playboy* magazine. As the audience heard the words "*Playboy* magazine" I held up a Superman comic book and flipped through so everyone could see cartoon pictures of the caped one.

"With these special spectacles Superman turned into Playboy." I put on a pair of glasses and suddenly the comic was magically now a *Playboy* magazine, complete with a sexy girl on the cover. Again I flipped through the pages, and this time everyone saw pictures of finely toned, scantily clad women. "But without the glasses it was Superman." I took off the specs and again the publication had a Superman cover with superhero pictures inside, and magically changed back to Playboy when the glasses were returned to my face.

"One time the barber said, 'Hey Steve your mom is coming...' I didn't get the glasses off in time, and Mom saw the best Hugh Hefner had to offer; the naked centerfold fell out of the magazine and...Have you seen this month's Playmate? She's a real pig!" I turned around the centerfold and it was a big picture of the Muppets character, Miss Piggy.

Here are some of my other favorite tricks from the Brook Farm Inn of Magic:

- For this first one, I have to credit Mother Nature with an assist. The top half of the Farm's back door had a frosted glass window; from the outside, after nightfall, it looked like a big white glowing square. Summer evenings a plethora of moths collected there, enabling me to occasionally share a charming mystery that simulated the creation of life. It was an easy matter to catch a big gray fuzzy moth and hold it by the wings, clipped between my fingers in a way that kept it hidden from the audience and allowed me to use my hands in a natural manner. Thusly prepared, I'd tear a tiny portion of a paper cocktail napkin into the shape of a moth. After a magical gesture the paper moth became real, spread its wings, and fluttered away.

- Another regular part of the act, one of our best bits, was Mr. Sheets's rendition of fire eating. The lights dimmed. A hush fell over the audience as Bob took his first gulp of a flaming torch. As he became more gluttonous, licking up the flames like a dripping ice cream cone, the crowd, convinced at last that he was not in danger, began to laugh. "You laugh now," Bob told them, "five thousand years ago you would have made me chief."

- This was a reverse pickpocket routine, but instead of a pickpocket, I was a "put pocket." A man from the audience joined me on stage and was astonished to discover that his sports jacket was full of sausages, a rubber fish, a plastic pig, a frying pan, a baby bottle, several bras, silk panties...and then suddenly a spoon fell out of the guy's sleeve and clattered to the stage. Following that came a fork and two knives. The man looked down confused— to all appearances he had stolen a complete place setting. Finally an avalanche of silverware rained to the stage, with a tremendous crash.

- Bob always knocked them dead with his Deck Stabbing. After having seven cards selected, the deck was spread face down and mixed over a tabletop. While blindfolded, Sheets would successfully stab each selected card in turn on the point of a knife. The last time he thrust his knife in amongst the scattered cards he would push the knife into the table top through one last card, which allowed him to dramatically tip the table over towards the audience whereupon all the cards would cascade onto the floor, the chosen card pinned to the table as to a target. When the card was plucked free it proved to be the last of the selected cards.

At the time, other than Siegfried & Roy, Bob and I were under the impression that we were the only male magic duo out there. That is, until that day in 1981 when Penn & Teller came to one of our shows. Relaxed and uninhibited, we swapped stories and our counterparts were friendly, funny, and comfortable to be with. The following day Bob and I went to see them perform at Ye Olde Renaissance Pleasure Faire in Cumberland, Maryland.

Rumor has it that Penn & Teller are still alive and flourishing in numerous stage, television and film projects, not only as performers, but also as writers, producers, and directors. My admiration of the hardworking daring duo's talent that began back in 1981 was immense, and they continue to be a refreshing influence on me now in 2015. In fact, how Penn & Teller helped launch Magicopolis in 1998 will afford a few tinkling paragraphs later in this chronicle.

PART TWO

WAY BACK

A LEADS TO B
LEADS TO C

I was pulled out of a hat. Others might say I was destined to be a magician. That it was fate. Supernaturally ordained. You might say it, but I wouldn't. When it comes to paranormal phenomenon, most magicians are skeptics, and I'm no exception. Yes, magic goes way back in my family. No, I don't believe in cosmic forces. Yes, I live my life amidst mysteries, miracles, and dreams.

My father's father (my grandfather Morris Spillman, whom I never knew) was a tailor in San Francisco. As the story came down to me through the years, one day in February 1910, my grandfather sewed some secret pockets in a magician's tuxedo. That magician was a type known in the trade as a dove worker. He made birds magically appear at his fingertips. Before the birds made their magical appearance, they were hidden in those tailor-made secret pockets.

That magician, the dove worker, was more than satisfied with my dad's dad's tailoring skills, and he showed his gratitude with more than money. Besides paying the bill, he taught my grandfather a simple magic trick with string. The old man loved that trick where two strings magically became one and showed it to everyone. He passed that love onto my dad, who passed that love onto me.

Same as my granddaddy, my father, Sandy Spillman, considered doing magic tricks a hobby. Dad was as good-looking as a movie star, charismatic, and happy-go-lucky, with watery gray-blue eyes. His voice was deep and resonant, his enunciation splendid, he was book smart, and had a wandering mind. When mom asked him to pick up milk and bread on his way home, he might show up a few hours late with a magazine. There was an aura about my father. I don't know how to describe it, but there was something so impressive about him that he commanded love and respect, particularly from strangers. Dad had more charm than ambition, more dreams than follow through.

As an on-air personality in early television, my dad's magic hobby came in handy. In the 1940s, my father was a radio announcer. At the end of the decade his radio station got into the talking picture box business when they started KPIX-TV, the first television station in Northern California. That's where my dad read the news, hosted chat shows, game shows, and did commercials.

I distinctly recall my first definite memory. Perhaps this dawn of a knowable past was so thunderously certain because it concerned my passion for magic. It's 1959, in San Francisco, and I'm nearly five years old. I'm seated on the couch in our family living room, a babysitter on one side and my infant sister, Susan, on the other. We're watching TV. The television was a huge piece of furniture...on top were the antennas that enabled reception, called rabbit ears, below was a tiny rounded screen. The black-and-white picture was fuzzy and jumpy, and so was I.

We were watching a program called *The Money Tree*. It was a game show, just like *Who Wants to be a Millionaire*, except this was a local Bay Area show sponsored by a neighborhood grocery store. Correct answers to odd and offbeat trivia questions won contestants a can of baked beans or a package of frozen peas, and the grand prize was an electric can opener. That's what local TV was like in the 1950s.

My parents were hosts of *The Money Tree* and they opened each show by warming up the studio audience. On that particular day, my mom and dad treated everyone to a little magic routine. We watched father tear up some tissue paper. He wiggled his fingers over the torn paper and said, "I want everyone to scream the magic words, 'Money Tree,' three times, and wiggle your fingers three times..." He unfolded the torn pieces of paper and they'd magically formed themselves into a hat. Dad put the funny hat, which looked more like a bonnet, on a man's head and continued, "Call me sentimental, but I'd like you to have this."

Mom and Dad in a fifties TV press photo.

As we watched the on-screen laughs and applause, my mom tore her own tissue paper as she spoke, "I'd like to make a magic hat for this handsome man's beautiful and distinguished wife. I want to hear the words 'Money Tree, Money Tree, Money Tree...' At the count of three... One, two, two and a half, two and three quarters, three!"

As she unfolded the papers the audience giggled, then laughed, and then applauded loudly. What mom held in her hand was made of tissue paper, but it wasn't any kind of a magic hat; it looked like women's bikini-style panties. To me they looked like my sister's diapers. Mom put the panties on her head, "Stop laughing, it's a hat!" Father chimed in, "Underwear is fun to wear. After this commercial break we'll be back to magically make this lovely lady a matching bra!" It was at that moment that I knew I wanted to be a magician. And if it wasn't, it should have been. The seeds of who I am now had been planted.

About that time, the Spillman name was becoming firmly entrenched into the KPIX culture. As the face of much of the station's original local programming, Dad felt secure in his steady solid little world as a San Francisco media personality. Among other station chores, he wrote commercial copy, newscasts, and together with Mom had created *The Money Tree*.

Ultimately, my parents moved the family to Los Angeles, where they had sporadic success as actors, writers, directors, hosts—whatever they could get their hands on, really.

Unfortunately, Hollywood life took a toll on my dad. He was sick of it, literally. He got an ulcer and was bedridden for a couple weeks. That's when he lit the flame of magic in me, which, to this day, has never gone out. He sat up in bed, his jaws sagging at first, his face pale, stubbled with beard hairs, and taught me the simple trick with two strings that his father, my grandfather, had taught him. What I witnessed that day was one of the great thrills of my life.

The instant he started teaching me, a transformation came over him or from within him; he was no longer a slumped man in bed suffering from an ulcer, but rather he was suddenly vital and strong as if nothing was the matter with him. He was a regal master mentor, majestically passing the baton, the magic wand, to his son. Nowadays the same sort of thing happens to me; if I'm ill and have a show to do, another set of reflexes takes charge and the ailments seem to vanish while I'm on stage. After that day, instead of Legos or little green army men, the only toys I played with were magic tricks.

I was six years old when I gave my first public performance. It was in Encino, at the Hesby Street Elementary School talent show. The auditorium was packed with kids and parents. Everyone was watching and listening to my every word. You could hear a pin drop. I was in the spotlight, looking sharp. Mom had dressed me in a homemade cape, a top hat, and a small moustache that was pasted on my upper lip. I can still smell the glue, which made my nose twitch, so as I had walked onstage I pulled off the moustache and stuck it above the fly on my pants. As I did that I noticed my zipper was down. I spun around to fix things and the moustache got caught in the zipper and was hanging out of my fly when I bungled, faltered, and thoroughly screwed up The Vanishing Hanky Trick.

What happened was that the hollow fake finger I was wearing fell off and landed in front of me on the floor, and the bright red scarf that had been hidden inside was hanging out. I tried to sneakily pick it up, stuff the hanky back inside, and put the fake finger back on my hand. I guess my hope was that no one would notice. But they did notice. Big time. Because it fell off again, I was a real smoothie. I screamed...

Me at six years old, ready for action.

"I hate you, fake finger. I hate you. I hate you."

The audience went into hysterics and I had a mini panic attack. I was marooned on stage with embarrassment. I tried to leave right that second, but I couldn't find the split in the curtain. To be a truly great magician you have to be able to improvise. I improvised.

"Someone let me out! Where's the key to the curtain?! I'm trapped, well there's only one way out..."

I had started to crawl under the curtain, when it occurred to me that I didn't want to leave my fake finger behind. It was a prized possession, and I made no secret about the fact that I wasn't leaving without it. Still on my hands and knees, I turned around, crawled over, and grabbed it.

"I'm not leaving without my fake finger. Don't laugh, this trick's hard to do when you're wearing a fake finger!"

The crowd exploded with applause and screams of laughter. And my six-year-old brain thought, *I did that. I made them laugh.* I felt something rise up in me, a sense of pride, accomplishment—and at the same time absolutely no sense of accomplishment. I wasn't any good, and I knew it. But that moment a realization came over me; getting laughs can get you out of a jam. It felt like when my mom had the tissue paper panties on her head, which at the time, I didn't know was a carefully planned accident.

I also didn't know that it's better for people to laugh with you instead of at you. But I knew I liked being on stage, and I liked getting laughs. And I wanted to feel like that again. I was hooked. Believe me, there is nothing that feels as good as standing, or crawling, on stage and hearing the laughter and applause of an audience. At the same time, there is nothing more humiliating during your very first show than reeking of dorkdom. I wanted so deeply to be good but didn't know how. I guess I had a little talent then, maybe no more than any other six-year-old, but a passion was developing.

A FIFTY-CENT DECK
OF CARDS

Father directed a low-budget *Tarzan* movie, and the sudden burst of affluence moved us from our modest Encino address to a better address in the next town to the west, Tarzana. Yep, Tarzan got us to Tarzana, named because the land was once a ranch owned by Edgar Rice Burroughs, the well-known author of the jungle stories of Tarzan the ape-man.

Our Spanish adobe structure was a stone's throw from a tall iron enclosure surrounding the old Burroughs mansion, on Otis Avenue, a road named for General Otis, the original publisher of the *Los Angeles Times* and the guy who sold the ranch to Burroughs. The rock-solid homes that comprised our immediate neighborhood were the oldest in the city and each had a front lawn and a eucalyptus tree or three.

At the time, the rest of Tarzana were more modern pricier palatial homes in the hills surrounding two golf courses, El Caballero Country Club and Braemar Country Club. Tarzana was mostly a community of affluent suburbanites, many of whom tipped caddies, drove Caddys, and sent their kids to snazzy private schools. I came to resent one of those rich kids who looked down his nose at me.

I was ten years old when I was a regular at Femia's Party Shop on Ventura Boulevard in Tarzana. The proprietor, Charlie Femia, was a wild old man who always wore a squashed hat, little round glasses, and a rumpled shirt with baggy pants and suspenders. When he was hawking magic tricks, he would point so that it looked like he was giving people the finger, as he would say, "It's not three dollars, it's not two dollars, it's only one dollar." Everyone used to laugh at the way he would point with his middle finger because they thought he didn't know he was doing it. I was never quite sure.

In anticipation of his weekly magic trick demonstrations as many as a dozen boys in my age group would gather around the magic counter. On top of the glass counter was a spinning rack of practical jokes. Fake Dog Doody, Squirting Flowers, Hand Buzzers, Fart Candy, and a little viewer that promised to show a photo of a naked woman that left a black smudge around your eye. Under the glass were trick cards and coins—Svengali Decks, Marked Cards, Folding Quarters, and Double Headed Nickels. On shelves behind the counter were bigger tricks made of plastic, plywood, glass, or tin—or a combination of all of those things: Egyptian Water Boxes, Zombie Balls, Chinese Sticks, Strat-O-Spheres, and more!

Each and every Saturday afternoon, when the crowd was at its peak, Femia would demo all the marvels. His presentations were peppered with jokes that would appear dated now, and arguably even back then, but he would still convulse us into helpless laughter with tricks that looked better than they sound—like the one with the funnel that looked empty which in fact had double sides filled with water that he held under a boy's ear. After the kid's arm was pumped up and down for a bit, water would apparently start trickling out of his ear.

"Boys, gather around, all five of you, and you Steve, that makes six," he'd say. "The world famous Dagger Chest completely encases my head. Ugh, this is a heavy sucker. Solid oak. Get ready, I'm gonna open the doors."

Femia opened the doors on the front of the box so we could clearly see his face.

"Peek-a-boo, now you see me. Now you don't."

On the word "don't" he closed the doors and started shoving tin swords through the box. The swords looked like they were going through his face, his skull, and his brains! When he opened the front doors, you could see the sword blades going through the box, but Femia's head was gone! He had no head, but we still heard him say, "Any questions?"

I could never afford a Dagger Chest. Like most of the other boys, every once in a while I'd buy a small pocket trick with magic coins or cards. But there was this one kid, Kevin Grant (name changed to protect the . . . innocent), who got an allowance that would support a family of five for a year in a third world country. He always had a sweaty fist full of cash.

"Mr. Femia, here's the money, gimme the Dagger Chest."

"Okay Kevin, let me show you how it works."

"I don't need no instructions, I'm a master magician. Here we go! I'm a blockhead!" As he shoved in the first sword we heard a bloodcurdling scream, "Aaaahhh! Help! Guys get this thing off me!"

The doors flew open and the secret mirror smashed on the ground. Tears, mixed with blood from a small forehead abrasion, mixed with saliva drooling from Kevin's mouth. We were definitely laughing at him, not with him. Kevin was a terrible magician. If he were really smart he would have called himself a comedy magician.

One Saturday Kevin turned his attention to me.

"Steve, I'm going on tour. Last week I headlined show and tell at my school. I was sooo good. My teacher arranged for me to tour all the other classrooms. It's like ten gigs!"

"So what's in your show?"

"You've seen all the stuff I've bought—The Egyptian Water Box, Strat-O-Spheres, Confetti Cans, and everything in between. My standing ovation encore is the Dagger Chest."

"Kevin, be sure to have some iodine and bandages handy."

"Plus my dad is printing posters. A lot of important people go to my school, and once everyone knows about me, I'll be starring on the *Ed Sullivan Show*.

"Ed Sullivan? Kevin, you're only ten years old!"

"Did you see The Jackson 5 on Sullivan last week? The lead singer is only eight years old. It's now or never, there's no chance if you haven't made it by ten!"

At the time I was almost eleven. Later, at home, over dinner, I was a wreck.

"Mom! I don't have any money to buy a Dagger Chest and an Egyptian Water Box so I can be on *Ed Sullivan*! It's now or never!"

She responded to this shocking announcement by study-ing my physical contortions, then felt my forehead. "Good gracious, Steve! You really are ill! Eat your broccoli; do you want more potatoes?"

"Kevin Grant has a super solid half hour of mystery that's gonna get him on *Ed Sullivan*. How am I going to buy all those big tricks when my allowance is only one dollar a week?"

My father knew just what to say, as he peered into my eyes. "There's more than one way to skin a cat. Remember Liberace? On *Sullivan* he drove a Rolls Royce on stage, wore a mink cape, and had a candelabra decorated with precious gems..."

"Could I please have the same allowance he gets?"

"And right after Liberace was Bob Hope. He didn't have anything but himself."

"I love Bob Hope."

"That's my point. Hope is funny. You like being funny. Plus you're good with your hands. Maybe you could do more with your Svengali Deck?"

Suddenly I was inspired like never before and cherished those tricky cards as though they were precious jewels. Two Saturdays later at Femia's I wowed the boys with my new Svengali Deck routine.

"I need someone who is handsome and brave to shuffle the cards. Okay, okay, I'll false shuffle them myself while I'm blindfolded. Now, without the sense of sight I'm going to impale the card Kevin just selected on the end of this screw-driver. Is that it Kevin? Now all the cards change to Kevin's card, but wait, now his card is gone, but here it is in my fly. And, oh, hey, it's still warm."

My new Svengali Deck routine was a smash success. Everyone laughed, applauded, and loved it, especially Kevin Grant. And I knew he was sincere, because he invited me to his birthday party, and he didn't invite even one of the other magic boys. Just me. And I knew what to do to make him happy on his birthday.

At Kevin's party, one by one the gifts were opened—an electric guitar, a leather jacket, and from me, a brand new Svengali Deck. Attached was a rolled-up parchment paper. With an old-fashioned fountain pen and India ink, in calligraphy, I had handwritten my entire Svengali Deck routine. I spent a week composing it, in which I confided several tidbits of information having to do with my super secret methods of handling the cards. I disclosed, among other things, each and every moment from what the audience sees, how to do it, and what to say, with a lot of personal tips, suggestions, and comments. I had poured my heart into that document and clearly remember the way the ink strokes ran in the many pen drawings of cards and hands. I wish I had that parchment today. It was a beautiful work of art.

The following Saturday, with triumphant pride I marched into Femia's. The store went silent when I stepped through the door. Even though all the usual suspects were there, no one greeted me, except for Kevin, who greeted me as if I had leprosy. He laughed in my face and, in front of all the magic boys, yelled "Don't invite Steve to your birthday party, he'll give you a fifty-cent deck of cards!" It was a comment that invited response, and had I had my wits about me, I should have said, "Go to hell you spoiled brat. You should have felt lucky I even came to your stupid party." But I didn't say a word. My tongue froze solid in my mouth.

I turned on my heels and marched out of Femia's, a little shriveled inside, jumped on my bike, popped a wheelie, then pumped the pedals for the ten-block ride home. Dad said, "This isn't a great tragedy. Get over it. You're okay." Mom sat me down with a toasted cheese sandwich, and I accidentally dribbled a little melting goo on my Svengali deck.

"You told me yourself, Kevin looks foolish doing magic tricks. No matter how much they cost, if he can't do those big tricks well, they aren't worth fifty cents. But writing a good story, painting a beautiful picture, or creating the ultimate Svengali Deck routine can make you feel like a million dollars."

That day way back when, I started feeling like an eleven-year-old millionaire.

Kevin, if by chance you happen to be reading this, I'd like you to know that fifty-cent deck of cards took me around the world.

THE FIRST TIME I ADVERTISED MY MAGIC SHOW

It was 1966 and I was a paperboy. Every day at the crack of dawn I'd get up, and I'd fold and rubber band seventy-four San Fernando Valley Green Sheet newspapers. I loaded the papers into two canvas bags that hung on the butterfly handlebars of my bike, a lime green Montgomery Ward version of the Schwinn Sting Ray complete with knobby tires, banana seat, and sissy bar. I then peddled like a mad man around my Tarzana neighborhood, throwing papers onto people's lawns, driveways, and porches. Then I'd ride my bike to school.

Some mornings, in addition to folding and rubber banding seventy-four papers, I was required to add an advertising supplement to the mix. While stuffing flyers for Jake's Jug, a neighborhood liquor store, it occurred to me that stuffing newspapers with a flyer advertising a certain boy magician would be a good idea. A perfect scheme, almost perfectly executed...

Using carbon paper, I made four smeary purple ink copies at a time, until I had seventy-four flyers with the following headline:

FAMOUS BOY MAGICIAN AVAILABLE FOR SPECIAL OCCASIONS.

As luck would have it, I got a call.

"Yes Mrs. Lewis, this is Steve the famous boy magician."

"Darling, I'm having a Beauty on a Budget party. It's like a Tupperware party, but I sell beauty products. It's my first party and I really want to impress the ladies and I think magic tricks would be great. Sweetheart, how much do you charge?"

Which brought us to our spirited negotiation. For some reason her question had caught me by surprise, and after a momentary pause, with a minimum of confidence, I spit out two words, "Three dollars."

"Honey, it's a deal."

And just like that I was on the road to fame and fortune.

The three giggly women and their hostess seemed amused with my tricks and they gave me a sitting ovation. When I tried to leave, Mrs. Lewis took me aside and whispered, "Darling, wait until the party's over. I'll pay you from the cash I get selling my beauty products."

So I'm waiting, the women are having a ball putting different lipsticks and mascara on each other, squirting each other with perfume and painting over the dark circles under their eyes. Then one said, "Oh girls, look at the time, gotta go." And quick as that the party was over.

Suddenly I was alone with Mrs. Lewis. She thanked me and started to clean up. When I asked for my three dollars she looked me right in the eye and said, "Darling, the ladies didn't buy anything, so I don't have the cash to pay you." Then she put her arm around my shoulder as she escorted me to the door.

"I think my work should be paid for. Don't you?"

"I am amazed! Truly amazed! Why, my dear child, Jesus never asked for money."

"But it's only three dollars."

"Look Honey, just take this rouge, if you want."

"What do I do with this?"

"Oh Sugarpie, you are in showbiz now, you need professional makeup! Please also take this foundation and eyebrow pencil with my compliments."

What a rip off! *And,* the makeup gave me a rash.

THE LEGEND OF CARDINI LIVES ON

In sixth grade I was a regular at a secret magic store in Hollywood. Not a street-level store with a sign—it was hidden upstairs in an office building. I took the world's oldest elevator to the second floor, then down a threadbare hall to Joe Berg's Magic Shop. That's where the late great Harry Blackstone Senior fooled me with a card trick, and where I first heard of Cardini, the superstar vaudeville magician.

The store's owner, Joe Berg, was a pudgy little man that never drank, never smoked, never wore a hat, and was a very clever inventor of magic tricks. He really cared for his customers, but at the same time he seemed to be the world's worst businessman. I'd often hear him say things like:

"I'm sorry, that's not for sale."

"No, this just doesn't fit your personality."

"...beyond your skill level."

"...isn't for you..."

I wanted a lit cigarette dropper, a device that hung under your coat and secretly fed lit cigarettes into your hand. It was a rusted used prop, covered in dust, but Joe wouldn't sell it to me because he thought I was too young to play with lit cigarettes.

Joe said, "No, no, no Steve. No can do! Eleven-year-old boys don't smoke cigarettes. It's wrong for you. Forget it. Go with this Appearing Bouquet of Feather Flowers."

"I'm not a girl. I don't want feather flowers," I think I said. "I want the lit cigarette dropper." After a few minutes of pleading, it was apparent Joe wouldn't change his mind, but I had a plan.

Every once in a while Joe had to take his wife to the doctor, or for some other reason couldn't be at the store. And then Joe's son, Ronnie Berg, was in charge. Ronnie would sell anything to anyone at any time. After a million visits, one day I walked in and Ronnie was minding the store. Here's how the conversation went with the man who introduced me to the brilliant work of Cardini.

Ronnie said, "...perfect for you Steve. When a young boy smokes it makes him look more mature and sophisticated, like a man of the world! And this lit cigarette dropper is in a class by itself! It's a handcrafted masterpiece created by an English artisan for Cardini. Cardini! The highest paid ever, superstar vaudeville magician. It's the only one of its type in existence."

I had no idea who Cardini was, but I was very excited. Cardini owned this, and he was a superstar! He touched it and then I touched it. Soon I'd be the highest paid superstar of magic. Then Ronnie elaborated.

"The late great Cardini was friends with my father, and on his deathbed, Cardini gave Joe this treasure. I wish we had another one so you could get a spare. But this is the one and only one on the face of the Earth."

When the deal closed I was trembling! I possessed Cardini's Very Own Personal Lit Cigarette Dropper! Cardini, the former vaudeville superstar! I thought, *It's like in the movies!*

Twenty-five years later at a Magic Castle swap meet I saw another lit cigarette dropper, identical in every way to the one I owned. And the guy said, "There's a great story that goes with that..."

"Let me guess, on his deathbed, Cardini gave Joe Berg this lit cigarette dropper. There's not another one like it." We both cracked up when I told him I got the same Ronnie Berg story. That Cardini must have been awfully busy on his deathbed.

What's even funnier and more significant to me is the fact that Ronnie gave me the deathbed story in 1967, but Cardini didn't actually pass away until 1973. When I think about it now, this incident was not only a valuable magical lesson on how to lie to someone's face, but it was also an inspiration for the title of this book. Of course, my lies are the lies that fool people into perceiving what I do as defying the laws of nature, not the lies used to profit from the sale of super secret gizmos.

The one and only time I used the cigarette dropper was when I was about thirteen. I had somehow gotten in with a group of guys who were a little older than I was, and more sophisticated. They knew a lot of teenage girls, and through them I got invited to a party at the house of the most popular one around. The girls were all several years older than me and I had secretly hoped that a cute female would fall insanely in love with me. Instead a cute girl asked me if she could bum a smoke.

Inside the dropper was a little battery with a glow plug that kept cigarettes burning so that when you made one appear you could instantly puff on it and real smoke would come out. I had the dropper hidden under an open vest above my waistband.

My left hand provided the perfect misdirection as my right hand secretly reached for a lit cigarette.

At the same fraction of an instant, with a deep breath I sucked in my stomach; as a result, a space opened at the top of my trousers, the gimmick jiggled, I fumbled, and the red-hot burning cherry of a lit cigarette fell down my pants and lodged itself in my underwear.

My privates were burning, I was uncomfortably wiggling around, and smoke was coming out of my pants. I was embarrassed, but fortunately the girls laughed and seemed to think my smoking pants and wiggly little dance were all part of the act. I had never had a more attentive or appreciative audience in my young career.

Not unlike my fiasco with the fake finger and hanky, again I survived a major gaffe. But the fact is, later I suffered with a big bubbly blister that stung when it popped. I guess Joe was right. I was too young to play with lit cigarettes.

PART THREE

BECOMING MYSELF

THE MAGIC CASTLE

Mom: "How did the audition go at CBS?"

Dad: "Hard to say."

Mom: "Every no just moves us closer to the next yes."

Dad: "When the casting director saw on my resume that magic was one of my special skills, he hooked me up with a guy that's opened a Hollywood nightclub for magicians. It's called The Magic Castle."

Mom: "I know what you're thinking, but we don't have money for nightclubbing."

Dad: "Put on your best dress. Tonight we're meeting the owners of the Magic Castle."

Halfway through seventh grade at Portola Junior High in Tarzana I got the news we were being downsized to a smaller home. Although my parents had recently sold a script to the cowboy series Death Valley Days—and had written, directed, and cast themselves as well as my sister Susan and me as a family magic act in an industrial film for the Revere tape recorder company—it wasn't enough to keep us in our Tarzana house.

Hey, we're in showbiz! Me and my magic family in an industrial film.

Again we moved one town west, to Woodland Hills this time, north of Ventura Boulevard on Keokuk Avenue near that old revered institution, Pierce College. I resumed seventh grade at another old revered institution, Parkman Junior High in Woodland Hills. I had been unable to find satisfaction in academic life. This, of course, was not the fault of the school, but all I ever wanted to do was get out of there. The fault lay within me, within my confused and magic-obsessed nature. I felt like a complete outsider, the only one of my kind.

For the most part, I didn't bother to even try to excel at school, and I spent most of my time daydreaming about tricks and jokes, talking to myself as I acted them out in my mind. This got me into a lot of trouble, and I became accustomed to it, I guess. I used to sit at my desk in class, doing card tricks. What better audience is there, than a couple dozen students who can't leave the room for an hour? My mischievous actions were rarely condoned, which encouraged in me a strong distaste for discipline.

To put it a bit mildly, my cards would often be confiscated or I'd deservedly be kicked out of class and sent to the Boys' Dean for being an interruptive disturbance, although I felt more like an amusing jerk than a bad boy. Mild corporal punishment was how they dealt with misbehavior. I'd be ordered to bend over and grab my ankles. The Dean picked up a wooden paddle that had holes drilled in it to minimize wind resistance, and I'd get a swift hard swat or two. "Next time you'll remember not to interrupt your class with card tricks." Then I'd walk out of his office rubbing my shoulder. I couldn't rub the place he'd swatted me in front of the other kids.

The Dean would call home to say that I was too busy doing tricks in class to learn anything, that my attendance was poor, that I was capable of doing better, and that I had better do better because I couldn't do worse. Next my mother would go into mild hysterics. She would look at me as if I were twinkle-eyed and naïve, telling me to keep magic as a hobby but not to let it interfere with my schoolwork, and then she'd beat me with the usual lecture on the importance of a good education.

"But I don't care about school. Magic is my life's work and I need to practice every chance I get."

My life plan was my mother's worst fear. Mom wanted me to have a career that would provide a secure life. All she ever wanted was for me to grow up and be comfortable. I felt proud. Magic was something I loved, it was in the arts, and not unlike what my parents were doing. Outside of my interest in trickery, I was just a know-nothing kid. She tried to reason with me, but reason never stands a chance against an obsession. I could only express myself with that old hand-me-down cliché, "Choose a job you love, and you'll never work a day in your life."

Mom said she and my dad had endured disappointments, just as nearly everyone in showbiz does. One of the things that kept her going was the hope that things would be financially more comfortable for her children. The first time I informed my mother that I was going to be a magician, she didn't get that I wasn't asking for permission. Rather, I was telling her what I was going to do.

"Think about it, Steve. Chances of big success as an actor, writer, or director are a billion to one. And there are far fewer opportunities for magicians than there are in any of those professions."

"I'm gonna be a magician."

"You need to have a safety net. Something to fall back on if your magic dream doesn't work out."

"My mind is made up," I said. "You'll stand up and cheer when you see me on stage."

"No," she said, "I'd have to sit down from the excitement."

Mom realized there wasn't much she could do to change my mind. My dad didn't encourage me to go into magic as a profession either. At this point in time magic was an almost forgotten hobby for him, until that miraculous day that changed both our lives, when my parents met Bill Larsen, his wife Irene Larsen, and brother Milt Larsen, the three force-of-nature founders of The Magic Castle. Everything really changed for me then.

The Castle is a huge old mansion in Hollywood and a portion of it had been developed by the trio as a private club for magicians and fans of magic, complete with a piano, a bar, a tiny showroom, and a bunch of old guys showing each other card tricks. The rest, as they say, is history. And if it really isn't history, it's magic. Going forward my mom seemed to be okay with the fact I would never turn back. I was a magician for life—good, bad, or blah. Plus my dad's life turned to magic. He was offered a job as a host at The Magic Castle. Not long after, he also became a manager. Later his acting skills made him the perfect candidate to play the Medium for the Castle's Houdini Séance show. Father was a triple threat at the Magic Castle and he worked there, full time, for the next sixteen years.

Thinking of my first days spent in the old structure, there were not too many teenagers hanging around. But that building, to a young aspiring magician in the sixties, was like the White House to a politician, or like leaving real life and walking onto a movie set. To me, it was the coolest place in Los Angeles, if not the entire universe. And I had a certain cachet at the Castle, partly because I practiced religiously (which is difficult to do when you're not religious) and could perform many difficult card sleights, and largely because of my dad, the host/manager/séance medium. Everyone always treated me with respect because they loved my father. I felt right at home with the senior citizen magicians.

The Castle was my home away from home; within its walls I met men who would shape and influence me throughout my life. It was the only institute of higher learning I ever graduated. Just to reassure you, I'm not saying that a college education is a complete waste of time. All the same,

I certainly preferred my own personal institute of magical learning to any college or university. For the first time I was accepted as an equal among adults, people with far more experience than I had, who recognized in me abilities and helped me to nurture them. As in any craft or profession, the more I learned, the more I realized I didn't know, and I was absolutely compelled to find out.

Every old guy carries within his own memory a special golden age. Then, when he becomes old enough to seem secure that no one will challenge him on it, he tends to make a shining legend of that time. In this case, however, it is a fact, and I feel ordained to tell you those years I spent in the mid-sixties to early seventies at the Magic Castle were a golden age. There was something in the air then, something that went away even before most of us realized it was there in the first place.

It was a largely dormant period in terms of work for professional magicians, both the supper club and vaudeville eras were long dead, and the Castle was the place to go when there was no place to go. It was a place to find a kindred spirit willing to compare the merits of controlling cards with the overhand shuffle as opposed to the double undercut or the pass. All the greats were there, and most were resourceful enough to find a way of easy living without work. Some of these Castle regulars were magicians when there was no radio, no television, no talking movies, when showbiz consisted of live shows. Every town in America had vaudeville houses and theaters and clubs and saloons, and they all had live entertainment and some of these men were magicians who were headliners.

These headliners I met during my wide-eyed time of questing were neither too big nor too busy to reveal to a young stumbler what was what in the world of magic.

A newcomer like me was eager to hear the tales they had told a hundred times, and my mentors were at that stage of the game where they felt closer to the past; their minds were museums of memories and all sorts of little thoughts turned up.

After a while I'd heard all those stories fifteen times, but the repetition was often fun. On rare occasions I'd be privy to stories that hadn't been remembered to that moment or had never before wished to be recounted. Only the memories of those present would keep them alive; some of those stories have been immortalized in this book. I was privileged to hear the contrasting talk of older men who had been on top, and that of heady young dreamers of fame.

The Magic Castle opened a door in my mind, and the potential for what a magician could do seemed limitless. It was a very exciting feeling. Other kids my age had heroes like Batman and Superman. I had The Man Who Fooled Houdini and The Man With The X-Ray Eyes, both real men named Dai Vernon and Kuda Bux, who I got to know very well personally along with Charlie Miller and Francis Carlyle. Each of the four was a magical icon. Many of the other early Castle members were to become well known in the trade; some were never to know the fame they deserved. But to me they possessed, all of them, greater attributes than renown. They were my friends.

Way back when, outside Bill's office on the top floor of the Castle, was the old library. I used to sit there, in a rustic antique chair, a chair that long ago had belonged to Dante the magician at his ranch in Northridge, which legend had it also once supported the posterior of trickster Howard Thurston, not to mention the aristocratic rear of illusionist Harry Kellar. It was the best chair I ever sat in, reading and dreaming and smelling the stale cigar aroma that lingered through the day from the nightly card games Dai Vernon, Kuda Bux, Charlie Miller, and Francis Carlyle played there. Smoking was not only permitted at the time, but rather it was practically required, and most nights the club was more overcast than a Santa Monica morning.

Aside from card-playing magicians, an endless parade of other diverse personalities drifted in and out of the Castle. I was so blessed to have watched this cast of characters. It was an incredible time. I craved their attention and by osmosis learned their lessons. Each one had his own trick, a nuance, a personal way of doing things, a lesson, a gesture, a story, a philosophy, an attitude...I was a sponge and absorbed something from each of them. All of it went into my mental file. Very gradually, right up until today, little bits and pieces that seemed to inherently fit me surfaced and worked their way into my performances, and the combination added to my personality gave me something new. Part of Carlyle's delivery, but not his words; the way that Miller would look at an audience after something amazing happened; a little sly, confident half-smile like Vernon—I began to store these gestures in my mind to eventually incorporate into my own routine.

The showroom held around twenty-five people and was called the Close-up Gallery. I had never seen anything so wonderful before, and I kept clapping long after everybody else had stopped. In that little theater I witnessed these seasoned talented performers doing sleight of hand with cards and coins and balls and ropes and handkerchiefs and silverware and I wanted to be one of them.

At fourteen, I appeared in the Close-up Gallery doing a single, twenty-minute show, on Sunday nights. At the time, Sunday was the only night those under twenty-one were officially allowed in the Castle. A few years later they started a Sunday brunch for the under twenty-one crowd and instituted a no-one-underage-in-the-evening policy. Despite the new rules, in 1973, starting at the age of eighteen, I worked the Close-up Gallery three shows a night, seven days a week, two to four times a year. It was a great way to learn my craft.

Leading up to my very first Sunday night show I hardly slept at night. I lay awake thinking about the excellent act I would do. All I thought of was the night of my debut. All the other days of my life, the ones that had been lived, and the ones that were to come, were just dates on the calendar waiting upon my very first show in the Close-up Gallery at the Magic Castle.

The man who introduced the Sunday night acts was a grumpy old guy known as Senator Crandall, although he was no more a senator than I was, but merely used the title to enhance his status. I'd read about him in the magic magazines, and before he introduced me the first time, he asked if there was something I'd like him to say about me. These were the words that gushed out of my fourteen-year-old mouth, "It's such an honor to meet you, Senator. I never thought the day would come when I'd be privileged enough to work with you." The Senator was a very sentimental guy. "Don't give me that crap, kid," he told me, "you'd just better be good."

I was, at the very least, watchable and perhaps rose above adequate; the problem was that I was so nervous that I began working faster and faster until my twenty-minute show only lasted ten minutes. But for the first time, I really felt like a professional. My act had a number of classic tricks including variations with cards like Cutting the Aces, Color Changing Deck, Cards to Pocket, and coin tricks such as Copper Silver and Coins Through the Table. I closed with my version of the Cups & Balls trick. Inspired by Andy Warhol's Campbell's Soup Can paintings, I developed a routine with a single Campbell's Soup can and a single cherry tomato. The little tomato appeared and disappeared under the cover of the can. The climax came when two large beefsteak tomatoes appeared.

This era also had its share of celebrities who liked having a place to see magicians do their thing. You might call them Magic Castle fans or cheerleaders. It was always a thrill to occasionally see TV personalities like Robert Lansing, Bill Bixby, and Bob Barker, or have a brief chat or show a trick to celebrities like Edgar Bergen or Buddy Ebsen.

During one of my very first shows in the Close-up Gallery, when I was fourteen years old, there was a guy in the second row on the aisle who seemed familiar. The whole audience seemed to be aware of his presence and where he was sitting. I recognized him and said out loud, "Were you at Eddie Shlepper's bar mitzvah?" He shook his head no and everyone laughed. After the show that dignified man came backstage to say hello. It was movie star icon Cary Grant!

I have many pleasant memories from the Castle's music room, where a baby grand piano is played by Irma, an invisible ghostly pianist. She plays musical requests and even answers questions with just the right song. Milt told me he adapted the invisible piano player Irma idea from an invisible harp player outlined in one of his favorite books, *Magic, Stage Illusions and Scientific Diversions* by Professor Albert A. Hopkins.

Both the harp and the piano require a hidden musician. The Castle's secret pianist was, and I think occasionally still is, a talented ivory tickler named Dave Bourne. From Dave's tiny secret workspace, he could see into the music room through a two- way mirror, and hear what songs folks requested through hidden microphones. So could I.

I spent some very special evenings in the little room with Dave. Sometimes there were as many as a couple dozen people jabbering away, drinking cocktails, and requesting songs. Other times, there was no one at all, or a couple of folks confiding secrets to each other, maybe flirting with some new acquaintance, whispering arrangements for a love tryst, or committing treason, unaware we were spying on them.

The most requested song was always "Happy Birthday" and when requests came for unknown tunes, Dave would slap the keys in a way that sounded just like a verbal "No." While the human player took a break, a flip of a switch would put the instrument into player piano mode. An empty birdcage sat atop the piano and served as a tip jar. When someone threw in a buck, I was allowed to operate the lever that made the perch swing and produced a canary tweeting sound, followed by Dave playing a few bars of the song "We're in the Money."

None of my friends from school were aspiring magicians. That was a peculiar profession, still is, if indeed it was a profession at all. To this day, just supporting myself by performing has always been to me major success as a professional tricky person. More than anything, the Castle made me feel like a magician. Before that, inside, I really thought of myself as just a guy who did tricks. I learned that one of the most puzzling creatures for the average person to understand is a magician. Even now, when I'm introduced to someone as a magician, they often ask, "So Steve, that's all you do, magic tricks?"

The first time I did a lecture for a group of professional magicians was at the Magic Castle. My opening line was, "So that's all you do, magic tricks?" There was a big laugh. I didn't have to tell the early part of the story. All the magicians there knew what I meant. This feeling towards magicians is not new.

Over the years several room additions and remodel work were done and today the Magic Castle is a world famous exclusive conjuring catacomb of multiple theaters featuring stage, parlor, close-up magic, four bars, a new library, and a restaurant that together entertain thousands of magic fans per week.

Nowadays I don't get the opportunity to visit the Castle as often as the old days. But when I do, I sometimes see my old self in the many new young magicians obsessed with our craft. And today the club attracts a new crop of famous faces that support magic and magicians, like Johnny Depp, Jason Alexander, and recent past Magic Castle prez, Neil Patrick Harris.

Not long after Dad started his tour-of-duty at the Castle, I accompanied him to a backyard barbeque at Brookledge, the Larsen family home. Bill fondly reminisced about shows he and Milt did with their mom and dad at some resorts way back when and how that afternoon's barbeque was part of a Larsen family tradition of hosting the magic community at their home. That tradition continues to this day at The Magic Castle. The only difference is that the Larsens moved most of their magic parties to a place where they could have a cash register. That's not my wit—the cash register line has been an inside joke between Larsen family members since forever.

MEN I HAVE LOVED, MY EIGHT FAVORITES

As a young man, my love life was robust. Besides the eight men, in my promiscuous past I've loved many women. There was Brigitte Bardot, Ann Margret, Raquel Welch, Jacqueline Bisset, Kim Basinger, Bo Derek, and Sharon Stone. I loved them all. I never met them, but I loved them. This chapter, however, is about eight men of the era I actually met and loved. They were all remarkable magicians I knew intimately during that golden age at the Magic Castle—the mid-sixties to early seventies. If you are a magician who was hanging around the Castle during those years, you might have your own eight favorites who deserve to be mentioned, and possibly you'll be adding them or replacing my list with those dudes.

I wrote dudes, but there was actually one accomplished dudette magician around, Diana Zimmerman. She was married to Dick Zimmerman, also a magician, and they were both very creative individuals who played an integral part in the Castle's advancement during those early years. Now I'm going to blab a little about Diana, then a couple other guys, before getting into my official list.

Diana was perhaps half a dozen years older than I, very attractive, and most generous with advice to younger magicians. She did a novel magic act with albums, those round pieces of vinyl, which was how we used to listen to recorded music. She manipulated LPs—long play albums—as well as singles—78s and 45s—not unlike some handled cards.

Her biz was making record albums float, diminish, and disappear, and for a finish she made a Victrola appear—a long out of production product from the Victor Talking Machine Company. Google it.

Just after I was too old to join, she founded a junior magic society at the Magic Castle for the under twenty-one set, which I believe she still heads up today.

Also to my dismay, as a young man I personally failed to get to know well or tutorially experience veteran performer and potential mentor Billy McComb, whose hilarious style as well as his superior magic had my utmost admiration. McComb moved to Los Angeles and joined the Castle fraternity in the seventies just as I was leaving the nest to relocate to Aspen. His artistry and the trajectory, consistency, and longevity of his career are attributes I aspire to.

Mark Wilson, a popular TV magician in the sixties and seventies, and one of the only regularly working guys in our craft of the era, was either too busy being on TV and doing corporate events for me to get to know well, or was repelled by my very existence, but influential nonetheless. Wilson was sitting on a bench outside the Castle waiting for his car, a Lincoln Continental, when I first met him. "Success in magic," Mark said, "is the sum of salesmanship plus talent. There's no shortage of talent, and there's no shortage of salesmanship. There is a shortage, however, of the combination of both talent and salesmanship in one person. You can have either one or the other and be a complete failure. You need both to succeed." Wilson then added, "I was talking about professional success. As far as one's personal private success is concerned, you need guts."

The master magicians on this list—colorful characters all—were what I consider to be my college professors, and the inspiration and guidance I got from them was tailored specifically for my consumption since they knew me personally.

They offered real knowledge that came from the experience of doing tens of thousands of shows. Above all, the one thing I learned most from my professors is that it is the magician's artistry and personality that give the audience an emotional response and sense of mystery, more so than the trick.

With the exception of Dai Vernon, the really interesting magicians to me were not handsome men. It was the characters who were different, who had unique quirks and problems to overcome, whom I, and I think audiences, liked best. These were extraordinary men, vital and forthright, and each had within himself great powers. There was also a bit of madness in these great magicians, and if they were to surrender it, they might be forfeiting their greatest asset.

When I arrived at the Magic Castle back in the Stone Age, these were the men who impressed me the most: Dai Vernon, Kuda Bux, Carazini, Tony Slydini, Charlie Miller, Senator Clark Crandall, Francis Carlyle, and Albert Goshman. If you're not exactly sure who these guys are, or were, it is only fair that I bring them sharply into focus.

Dai Vernon—"The Man Who Fooled Houdini" didn't fool The Great One once or twice, but rather he did it seven times in a row with a single card trick. Houdini boasted that if he saw a trick performed three times in a row he would be able to figure it out. Vernon then showed Houdini the same trick over and over and over. Each time Houdini insisted that Vernon "do it again." Finally Houdini's wife and friends said, "Face it, Houdini, you're fooled," which gave birth to Vernon's legendary designation.

Mr. Dai Vernon, head of the class of my personal heroes, was a dapper man with one of the two finest heads of silver-white hair at the Magic Castle—the other one belonged to Bill Larsen. Dai also had a silver mustache larger than one of his eyebrows but not quite as large as the two, and eyes that sparkled with an imperial confidence. When people say, "He was in a class by himself," they are talking about Vernon. Dai adored anyone who took a serious interest in sleight of hand and spent a large part of his life counseling and advising them with a dignified reserved indulgence.

He was a man who had always lived his life by his wits, and made friends everywhere and in all social climates—a very skilled raconteur with a vast repertoire of interesting anecdotes. I spent many enjoyable hours sitting with Vernon listening to him relate countless stories about the legendary magicians he had known. He would speak with the freshness one has for yesterday morning's happenings of celebrities he encountered like Billy Rose and various Rockefellers, Vanderbilts, Astors, and Roosevelts—stories about actors, crooked gamblers, circus folk, pickpockets, vaudevillians, and carnival grifters. I didn't know about any of those people; they were all new to me.

Dai Vernon and me in a manly embrace.

He was in his seventies when we met, and he lived to be ninety-eight years old, passing away in 1992. Probably the greatest contributor to the art of close-up magic who ever walked the earth, due to his extraordinary knowledge of and skill at sleight of hand, everybody affectionately called Dai Vernon "The Professor."

And The Professor had a nickname for me: Spill, short for my real last name, Spillman. He affectionately said he dropped the "man" because I was a boy magician. Spill. Vernon called me that, boy and man, all his life. The nickname stuck and eventually became my legal name. Funny, when Vernon first called me a boy magician, I felt like a man. Now, as a sixty-year-old magician, I feel like a boy.

Like me, The Professor started the study of magic when he was six years old. "I wasted the first six years of my life," he was fond of telling people. Having an interest in magic since we were small boys was all we really had in common. Among aficionados and experts in the field, he became the all-time single most world-renowned innovative artistic genius of magic that others wrote books about. I became a working guy who had to write his own book about himself. Sure it's best to have one's vanity served by others. But when all else fails, you do it yourself.

Before making Hollywood his permanent home, Vernon spent a lot of his life traveling all over the United States of America looking for card cheats, even arranging to interview ones who were jailed convicts because he felt the sleight of hand used by gamblers was superior to that used by magicians. His rationale was that a magician might get away with something sneaky because in a show one can misdirect by word or gesture and do anything within the limits of acting. Even if the audience saw something fishy they might be polite, take it in stride, and not mention it. But at a card table, where people were betting money, you're under the closest observation, and players generally are not polite if they see something suspicious. If a gambler cheated by using a secret sleight, he/she had to be very clever.

Vernon had a way of meeting any crooked gambler he wished to know and of winning that person's confidence, learning their methods, and applying them to his magic. An entire book, 2005's *The Magician and the Cardsharp* by Karl Johnson, was written about Vernon's search for a gambler who invented a sleight known as the "center deal."

The Professor was perhaps the single most influential card magician of the twentieth century, partly because he used card cheat sleights with which other magicians were unfamiliar, but also because he could take a second-rate trick and turn it into a masterpiece. Vernon twisted, changed, and made things more logical and more magical. Whatever trick he did became his own.

Besides tricks with cards, he is credited among magicians with inventing or improving many other standard close-up tricks with coins and other small items. The "standard" Cups and Balls routine is his, and his 6-ring "Symphony of the Rings" remains one of the most popular Chinese Linking Rings routines in use to this day.

The Castle became a landmark for magicians, hallowed ground, and that fact was accelerated by Vernon's arrival. Magicians around the country started moving to Hollywood to be near him. Old magicians came to see Vernon before they died and young magicians came to see him before he died.

Nearly every Wednesday between 1969 and 1973, I ditched school and hitchhiked (traveling by thumb was then the popular teenage mode of transportation) to the Magic Castle. The Castle wasn't open in the afternoon, and therefore the steady flow of tricksters who started to move to LA to be near Vernon were nowhere to be found, so I had The Professor mostly to myself. I'd sneak in through the kitchen and go straight to the music room in time to meet my guru, Dai Vernon, who would be finishing up his piano lesson—given to him by Ray Grismer—a retired teacher and expert magician himself, who traded piano lessons for sleight of hand instruction. I was there for the same reason, lessons in sleight of hand.

Vernon was very generous with certain secrets if he was convinced you had a genuine interest. If I mentioned how much I admired a trick he performed, he taught me the rudiments. I practiced the sleights, came back, showed him, or I had rearranged the sleights and made them into my own trick. I'd ask him not how good, but how bad he thought it was. I'd say, "Don't tell me if I'm good. Tell me when I'm bad, criticize me severely." Sometimes he liked it or said the plot of the trick was confusing, or it needed some misdirection to hide a secret maneuver.

If you practiced and learned, he gave you more and more. I learned dozens of different methods of palming, forcing, controlling cards, false deals, false cuts, false shuffles, double lifts, the pass, the hop, and the shift. Like jazz, these techniques could be combined in numbers of ways to create different tricks, I learned.

The Professor helped me become a dedicated craftsman, and encouraged me to experiment and explore and try to find my way with trial and error. And no matter how foolish I might have looked trying to do a trick or how poorly I might have performed some sleight, Vernon would push me on the next attempt to be more focused, more confident, and more relaxed. And his training was far from just mechanical—he taught me how thought and soul find their way into sleight of hand. He looked at playing cards as living, breathing beings.

Often the party moved to one of several nearby coffee shops; sometimes Vernon supplied transportation. He was still driving his old MG convertible with the leather seats and the walnut gearshift back then—it was always an adventure when we pulled away in a cloud of carbon monoxide. He never jumped a curb or grazed a tree, but it seemed to me that The Professor was often narrowly missing various things, like pedestrians. Never without his dashing nature, Vernon would look at me and nod confidently whenever we almost collided with something or someone.

Dai had a monthly column, "The Vernon Touch," in *Genii Magazine*, a periodical for magicians published by Castle founder Bill Larsen. Of all the great qualities Vernon had, and there were so many more than I have room to share in this book, there was one thing that set him apart from everything else. He really thought I had a future as a magician, and he wrote complimentary things about me in his column.

Those kind words sprinkled throughout "The Vernon Touch" led to a small magic dealer publishing a little book of my original tricks. Even though I was still a teen, as a result of that publication in 1973, *My Hands Can Be Yours*—a bad title with which I went along—I was invited to perform my close-up act and lecture to other magicians at a couple of national conventions.

About five years ago I received an email that read: *I recently attended an auction and bought a collection of magic books. Inside a copy of* My Hands Can Be Yours *are the words "Property of Dai Vernon," would you like to own it?* When I look at Vernon's familiar fancy handwritten block-lettered autograph in that book now, it brings back memories of our visits in the happy times of long ago. Sometimes The Professor would gaze upon me as I held a deck of cards and seem to be reliving his own early ambitions to be a magician. Vernon liked to sip brandy, puff on cigars, and discuss yesterdays, usually with a little grin on his face, the sort of half-smile that seemed to say, "I know something you don't know," which was always true.

Kuda Bux—"The Man with the X-Ray Eyes" covered each eye with a half-dollar, on top of which he put soft bread dough balls which he squished into his eye sockets, put strips of surgical tape over the dough, wrapped bandages around his head, followed by multiple layers of thick cloth napkins, and yet somehow the master mystifier still was able to see.

With all that stuff wrapped around his head he looked like the "Jack" character from the Jack in the Box fast food restaurants, but without dots for eyes and the line for the mouth. In that condition he fired a rifle at targets indicated by a volunteer, duplicated handwriting or drawings, played tic-tac-toe on a blackboard with a spectator, added columns of numbers, read aloud from books, and described accurately the contents of purses, wallets, and coat pockets. It was he who drove, blindfolded, through city streets in search of a hidden needle.

Then, after each and every performance, he mislaid his cigarettes and lost his glasses, and couldn't find them. Without the blindfold, he looked like a very dark-skinned Pakistani cross between Jamie Farr from the old "Mash" TV series and Wolfman from old horror movies. He smelled of curry and tobacco, had deep-set eyes, big bushy eyebrows, and had lots of hair growing on and out of his ears—not little tufts, but full crops that he brushed back and blended with his full of head of hair.

Over the course of his career, Kuda was a magnificent charlatan and mystic of esoteric skills who had been many things in many places. He was a master of thought transference, a clairvoyant, a firewalker, could stop his pulse at will, toured with his own full-evening magic and illusion show, and he had the newspaper clippings in his scrapbook to prove it.

I spent some time turning the pages of the scrapbook. Several newspaper articles written in foreign languages were pasted in. There were both English and American ones from the 1930s depicting Kuda walking across burning hot coals—that's over fifty years before Tony Robbins and others of his ilk popularized the pastime as a symbol of students' courage and personal empowerment. Bux's feet were checked before and after the fire-walking demonstration to verify that no protective chemicals, topical creams, or herbs were used. "There's nothing to it," he told me. He said moving quickly with self-confidence was the secret. "I think that's true of a whole lot of other things, too," he added. "Moving quickly with self confidence."

That was definitely a quotable quote, but unlike Vernon, he certainly wasn't forthcoming about many of his other secrets. I once said to him, "Kuda, I'd give five years of my life to learn your x-ray eyes act." He answered, "Would you indeed? I gave all of my life to do that." What a kick in the nuts—yet for the remainder of his life, his was one of the acts I still admired most, but the secret to his mystifying x-ray eyes was never revealed.

Sadly and ironically, in the last years of his life "The Man with the X-Ray Eyes" suffered a gradual loss of his eyesight. The last time I saw him perform, he was legally blind from advanced glaucoma, but wearing his elaborate blindfold,

Kuda Bux was still able to read the tiny serial numbers on my dollar bill.

The firsthand reminiscences of Mr. Bux became fixed forever in my memory. He was not boastful or given to swaggering. Rather he spoke with a frank exactitude concerning his many feats, neither praising himself nor belittling. A man who walks barefoot on thousand-degree coals is a realist even if he mostly deals in trickery.

I vividly remember the most important magic lesson I learned from Kuda. He said to me there was one "... pure magic moment in your show tonight. Do you know what it was?"

I had no idea what he was talking about. "Was it the moment when the first big tomato appeared under the soup can and..."

"No," Kuda interrupted.

"Was it when the coins vanished from my left hand and appeared in my right?"

"No," Kuda interrupted again.

I was quickly out of guesses. Evidently, a pure magic moment had gone right by and I'd never spotted it.

I had done a trick where a selected card was lost in the deck. When I made it appear and said, "Here it is," it was the wrong card. Next I inquired, "What was your card?" then wiggled my fingers and the wrong card magically changed to the right one. A very standard card trick plot...

But on this particular occasion, when asked, the guy named another wrong card, then corrected his error and named the right one. When he named the wrong card, I really believed I'd made a mistake and it showed on my face, but when he named the right one the relieved look on my face also showed. Then it occurred to me to make things right with a little magic.... Those few seconds encompassed the pure magic moment.

I couldn't immediately repeat those looks on my face that made the whole routine look realistic, but when Kuda pointed this out, I understood, and in the future strove to get myself again into a state of not anticipating what was next. Easier said than done. It was a little detail, but as I learned, of such details are great performances made.

Carazini—They say Carazini's real name was Jim Williams. The same first name as Jim Carrey, and Carrey sounds a little like Carazini, and this guy had a command of the same sort of rubber-faced characterizations that Jim Carrey is famous for.

Carazini had wrinkled fluttering eyelids, a pencil-thin mustache on a long lip, and his jaws worked constantly, whether or not he was speaking. His thrashed old black fedora hat, a size too big, was perched upon slicked back black hair. I admired what he did and it made a lifelong impression on me. Carazini was prepared to do his act at the drop of a hat, any time, anywhere, and that's what he did.

At the Castle, he might perform in the lobby, outside in the driveway, or at the bar, in a doorway. And he didn't need an introduction, didn't need a table, didn't say anything, didn't use any music, and the few props he used were in his pockets.

Carazini portrayed a lovable lush who had a few too many drinks. Not falling-down drunk, but inebriated enough that you believed it when he first lit a cigarette that bobbled on his moist lower lip—and then he accidentally swallowed both it and the lit match, and started to burp smoke. Between multiple burps of smoke, he'd belch up other things, like strings of silk scarves and dozens of eggs. His performance of the act was perfection—nothing ever went down the wrong pipe, he never made any gurgling sounds, sneezed, wheezed, got hiccups, choked, hurled, or coughed up a loogy.

When speaking with him it was hard to tell if he was staying in character by pretending to be a little drunk or if he really was, because he was always on. While we were in conversation I watched him put a match in his mouth and try to light it with a cigarette. Often Carazini would bend a spoon into the shape of a pipe and start smoking it. "Here Steve, you keep this as a good luck charm." He handed me a wet bent spoon by the handle, which had just been in his mouth.

On another occasion, I was forced to endure the story about his gallstones, which he carried around in a small bottle.

The man was, in my opinion, a talent who exhibited such extraordinary timing and subtlety, Carazini should be recognized as one of the great comic performers of the time...make that all time. The Magic Castle was only a burp in the road on his way to a career as a star specialty act, performing between nude female dancers at the world famous Crazy Horse Saloon in Paris.

Recently I found the old bent spoon Carazini had given me as a good luck charm more than forty years ago. My wife Bozena didn't know what it was and when I wasn't looking she threw it out.

Tony Slydini—The unique thing about Slydini, a genius sleight of hand innovator, teacher, and a performer, was that he did not have a set sequence of tricks. Instead he allowed the audience and the situation to determine his program. In particular, his impromptu after-dinner performances using whatever was on the table as props were absolutely astonishing.

Slydini had an enormous ego, but not offensively so. He talked much of himself and couldn't believe there would be an empty seat in the Castle's tiny Close Up Gallery when he was performing. Once, when I was in the audience, there was one empty seat in the front row. He just could not stand to see that empty seat. After his first trick, he stopped the show and said, "Ladies and gentlemen, I'd like you to take a minute and bow your heads in a moment of silence for this person who isn't with us right now. I don't know what happened to them, but they must be dead, or they never would have missed the great Slydini."

Slydini was an Italian boy, an Argentinian teenager, who as an adult mostly lived in New York, except for the year he spent at Hollywood's Magic Castle between 1969 and 1970.

His head always leaned a little to one side or the other, he spoke with his hands as much as his voice, and he talked from one side of his mouth, as though the opposite side were buttoned. He also smiled the same way, with only one side of his mouth (the other side was tight-lipped). At least once, in the unsmiling side of his mouth, I think I saw him carry a toothpick.

More often than not it was difficult to understand what he was saying, but oddly enough, whenever he performed, or talked about himself, his enunciation became not only quite distinct but elocutionary in quality. Slydini didn't have an accent until he came to the states, but his soft-spoken broken English had an original tone and sound, and so did his brilliant misdirection.

Misdirection is what magicians call the skill of focusing an audience's attention on one thing in order to distract its attention from another, and at this, Slydini was absolutely masterful. He so completely captured one's attention that they were prevented from discovering how he did what he did. Nothing exemplified this more than his Paper Balls Trick, a version of which is in my working repertoire to this day.

In this trick, the volunteer closely watching Slydini couldn't see what was going on, but the rest of the audience could. Slydini crumpled one paper napkin after another into little balls and made each one disappear, one at a time, before the participant's eyes. Every time, the audience saw that Slydini tossed the ball over the guy's head, but the helper was continually amazed and couldn't guess the secret.

His force of personality when it came to misdirection was so strong that a person who had a paper ball tossed over their head was convinced that paper ball slowly, magically dematerialized into thin air.

Normally magicians try not to overuse any certain secret method or technique for fear of getting caught red-handed. But because of Slydini's superlative skills at misdirection, he was able to sort of overuse a technique, called "lapping," to weave numerous miracles.

Lapping is secretly ditching small objects into your lap while seated at a table. Slydini could also secretly retrieve and exchange objects from his lap and you would never know it. Utilizing his amazing misdirection together with his lapping technique, Tony could tear a cigarette apart and put the paper on top of the loose tobacco in his hand and magically the cigarette would restore, then *bam*, it was back to a little pile of loose tobacco again. He would change salt to pepper and pennies to silver dollars.

I went out to an elegant dinner with a bunch of magicians and Slydini was the guest of honor. The great Tony Slydini blew everyone away all night doing tricks. Even waiters and people from other tables were watching. Spoons changed to knives, bread crumbs assembled themselves to a dinner roll, granulated sugar fused into cubes, and napkin balls appeared and disappeared under the bread basket. The show went on and on and on and Slydini was a king.

When we got up to leave I happened to glance under the table; the floor was covered with trash. Slydini had done tons of tricks during dinner and they all ended with him secretly tossing stuff into his lap and then onto the floor. Scattered under the table were wadded up napkin balls, bread, sugar, silverware, carrots, a salt shaker, a shot glass, a cream dispenser—you name it. It was like someone dumped a garbage pail on the floor. I wondered what the busboys must have thought when they found all that stuff?

Charlie Miller—Charlie Miller, Charlie Miller, Charlie Miller, was a man who liked to see his name spelled thrice, signed his name thrice, and when introduced he would say his name thrice. But he asked his friends to call him Chuckie, and when angry, referred to himself in third person, as Mad Dog Miller. He was a soft-spoken, introverted, timid sort. When he became your friend, you were buddies forever and he treated you with an almost fatherly kindness. By all accounts, including his own, he had never smoked or tasted liquor, and never cursed, told, or listened to any dirty jokes or off-color stories. In front of an audience he was charm personified.

Plump, with a pasty complexion, cherubic face, sparse light hair, and twinkly eyes, Charlie looked like a partly melted snowman. His skill with cards was equal to that of Vernon, and like Vernon he mastered sleights used by card cheats, but Miller was also a master at what we magicians refer to as stand-up, parlor, or cabaret magic—tricks done for larger audiences than what we call close-up and smaller than stage magic. Most professional magicians fall into this category.

Miller was Mr. Charisma when he performed the Chinese Rice Bowls. He said one time the band didn't show, so he provided his own accompaniment by whistling, which he'd been doing ever since. Chuckie showed two china bowls and wiped them with a little towel. One was filled with rice and the two were placed mouth to mouth.

Charlie would whistle his original tune; when the bowls were separated the rice magically doubled in quantity. The bowls were put back together, more whistling, the rice vanished, and in its place was cool clean water. Having heard him whistle his score so many times, I knew it well, and once started to whistle along with him. Horrible idea.

I could not sing the notes of the musical scale, but boy could I whistle! Not good, but shrill and loud. Charlie didn't miss a beat; he shook his head in a way the crowd thought was hilarious, kept whistling, and the magic continued. After the show I puckered my lips and began to whistle. Chuckie arched one eyebrow and chuckled a kinda nervous chuckle. Not a happy one, but a chuckle that sounded as though he couldn't think of anything else to say or do—reading between the lines it cured me of ever doing anything that might distract attention from another's performance, even if that interruption was meant fondly, like my whistling was. Nowadays that old tune, long forgotten, sometimes springs to mind. The melody rises from the past as songs oftentimes do and I recall in clear detail the lesson learned from my stupid whistling.

Holding up an empty hand, Charlie would say, "Imagine I'm showing you an invisible spool of thread," and, unwinding some nonexistent thread, would ask, "Do you see it?" Two volunteers pretended to hold the ends of long invisible thread, "Don't drop it." Chuckie placed a pencil on his hand, so the point extended over the end of his fingers and the eraser end was in his palm. He placed the tip of the pencil over the imaginary thread. "Now, gently lift the thread and see if you can move the pencil." They both moved their end of the nonexistent thread and the pencil magically moved upward as if being lifted by the imaginary thread.

Having seen Slydini make a big deal about doing a show with one empty seat in the Close-up Gallery, I was surprised when I saw Charlie perform there with a half-dozen empty seats and only about fourteen people in the audience. He worked his heart out in one of the finest performances I'd seen, and those fourteen lucky ones in the audience will never forget it. Neither will I. When I mentioned the Slydini incident, he said gently, "You know, Steve, when someone comes to see you, he's entitled to the best you've got, even if he's the only one in the audience." That night I vowed to never fail those who came to watch me perform. I like to think this is one promise I have kept.

In the beginning I would get flop sweat before every show. I used to think that nervousness would disappear, but Miller cautioned me against that. He said that when your nerves disappear, it's time to get out of the business. He was probably right. Fear is a good motivator.

Chuckie was meticulous about writing his monthly column called "Magicana" in *Genii Magazine*, the same periodical for magicians in which The Professor had featured me. One Magicana was devoted to a card sleight I devised called the Push Thru Change.

Having contributed to other magic publications throughout my teenage years, I knew the drill. What might take a couple of hours to translate into print elsewhere took Miller and me days. I performed my creation for him dozens of times, and he'd watch it from every possible angle. Laying on his back to my left, standing on his toes to my right, looking from behind me over my shoulder, and so on. Chuckie was both respectful and a straight shooter with his comments and critiques.

"Now try it with your fingers on top and thumb on the bottom to hide the elongation of the card during the change...instead of palming the extra card at the end, see if you can secretly leave it face up in the deck." By the time my little doodad saw print, it had been reworked by Charlie into a masterpiece.

Late in life Miller started a new career as a cruise ship magician. He enjoyed entertaining passengers onboard, and developed an interest in ballroom dancing, which kept him in contact with the ladies. As if the lady thing wasn't enough, I asked him, "Why is it cool to be a dancer?" Chuckie's answer was clear, "Because no one tells you off for having too much attitude."

Senator Clarke Crandall—The senator was a tall, heavyset, sarcastic, condescending guy, with a Salvador Dali waxed mustache, who always had a crooked little rum-soaked cigar in his mouth, and was not a real senator. His moustache wiggled as he talked and his eyes had two definite expressions; one was out-and-out mischief and the other plain lechery. Although the senator never swore, was never overtly graphic, and never exposed himself in public, he liked to label his shows X-rated, which I guess was true compared to the humor of other Magic Castle magicians. When I first met him he passed along to me the advice he said his father gave to him as a young man, "Son, try everything in life but incest and folk dancing."

The guy spoke in a gruff sort of under-his-breath way and sprinkled his performances with a lot of double-entendres. When he did the Cut & Restored Rope trick he'd ramble along in a stream-of-consciousness style: "It's an ordinary rope, just like you'd find at home in any bedroom...I did this trick on a cruise ship...where I learned women and seamen don't mix...when my ship finally came in, my pier collapsed..."

His rendition of the classic Cups & Balls trick, "...uhh, I got my balls screwed up...please grab hold of my magic wand..." and he would mumble about unrelated topics like octopuses that made love to bagpipes, clams that made love to castanets, before taking a big pocket watch out of his fly to check the time, then putting it back, and zipping up.

Part of his old grouch character was that he took umbrage at absolutely anything that was said. If someone said, "Happy Birthday," Crandall would reply, "What's happy about it?" or something equally grumpy. He talked down to people, and they liked it. "I'm not too crazy about you as an audience, but I'll do you a favor and show you a couple of tricks." If someone were amazed and exclaimed, not really expecting an answer, "How did you do that?" The senator would address the question, "It is part of my philosophy never to discuss matters of state with a commoner."

He said he had nothing against the people in his audience individually, it was just when they gathered that he didn't like them. To Crandall, everyone was a spoiled child, the guy insulted men and women alike, ogled sexy girls, and when he finished with a volunteer in his show, often they left unaware that there was a big chalk X mark on their back.

Crandall had absolutely no inhibitions about himself. He talked freely and colorfully, and to me his magic was poetic. Among my favorite tricks he did was the Six Card Repeat. He'd slowly count six cards, and didn't seem to notice, apparently by accident, that a few cards fell on the floor. When Crandall counted the cards again, there were still six. This went on and on and on until the floor was covered with cards, but there were still six cards in his hand. I guess it was no accident.

One day I ran into Clarke at Berg's Magic Shop. He asked if I wanted to tag along while he went downstairs to the old Woolworth's on Hollywood Boulevard to get some props for a trick he was working on. At the notions counter he perused the thimble collection, trying various ones on his finger and then putting them in his ear. "May I help you?" the saleslady asked. After a breath, he responded, "Yes. Please. My name is Senator Crandall and I'm looking for a thimble that will fit in my ear." The lady walked away a little disgusted and confused.

Senator Crandall was the most ornery lovable man I have ever known. I did not quite understand him...then. He hid none of his faults from the world. In fact, he hid nothing except perhaps what he planned to do with those thimbles.

Francis Carlyle—Picture a small ball of a man. With his short neck and pudgy body, he looked like a turtle that had somehow got out of its shell and was standing upright and walking around. He had a squirrel-like face, red-veined nose, a fiery temper, and a thick, punchy New York accent. When speaking loudly he would open his jaws until I had an oral surgeon's view of his throat and often spit in my face when he talked, but I didn't care, because he was one of the stars of magic. He was also a fan of mine when there weren't many others.

One of Carlyle's missions in life was not to bore or be bored. He muttered and spewed and cackled, coughed and wheezed and acted like he expected five thousand a show but always settled for somewhere in the high two figures. The man had a blunt sense of humor, and was a superb sleight of hand artist whose tricks never beat around the bush—they were always right to the point. He was also a lot of other things—none of them were shy.

Most of all, though, I loved watching him steal watches. In the course of showing someone a coin trick, he was able to gain possession of their wristwatch without their knowledge. At the end of the trick Carlyle would ask, "Can you guess whether the coin is head or tail? If you do, I'll give you a little prize." The prize was the volunteer's own watch, and the surprised look on the helper's face was always priceless.

During another great trick, Carlyle would twist a dollar bill into a little cone and use it to cover a stack of quarters on the back of a woman's hand. The quarters seemed to penetrate her hand and fell one at a time onto the table. When he removed the dollar from her hand, you'd see four pennies there. He'd say, "Sales tax!"

He was also a master at repeatedly fanning cards in a way that made the deck appear to shrink gradually into nothingness. He'd fan a normal deck of cards several times, and with each fan the cards repeatedly diminished, to half, then a quarter, then an eighth, and finally one sixteenth the original size. Then the deck vanished altogether.

Francis loved classical music, particularly Chopin played solo on piano, and listened constantly on a tiny cassette tape recorder in his apartment at the Nirvana, a building where a lot of the old timers like Miller and Crandall also lived. He seemed to find some great escape in the music as he shuffled a deck of cards. I remember his face losing its anxieties, he became serene as he shuffled, and he closed his eyes.

Once while visiting him, I saw him play chess with no board. The two men memorized the positions of all the pieces and spoke the moves to each other. Not a joke, it was a real game.

Francis was one of the first to do the Sponge Balls trick and the guy who taught it to one of my top eight favorites, Albert Goshman, who fashioned his performance of it into a masterpiece. Everybody wasn't doing it in the old days because you had to cut the balls from foam rubber or natural sponge. It was difficult and time-consuming to make a nice round matched set. Goshman came up with a way to mass-produce them.

I was with Carlyle when he was handed one of the first manufactured sets. "Here you are, Francis," Albert cried out as he presented the thin box containing four little sponge balls, "I wanted you to be the very first one to own a set." Carlyle was amazed, happy, and depressed all in the course of a minute or two. He couldn't believe how uniform the balls were and that they could be made in any size—and how well they handled. Then he became angry and depressed when he realized this unique trick would become widespread.

His frustrations, torments, impulsive actions, and stubbornness could be colorful, but he also had as short a fuse as many short men have. People would literally shiver until they laughed when he erupted in a rage. You could love him profoundly and hate him entirely at one and the same instant. Many examples spring to mind, but here's one that's seared into my memory. Carlyle had a little finesse with a move we magicians call the Double Lift—secretly holding two cards so they look like one—and he liked to fool magicians with his subtle variation on this sleight. My friend and fellow card trickster Randy Holt, who had seen him do this before, and knew the gag, as a practical joke, sabotaged his efforts. Francis wasn't amused.

"Feel the corner, just one card..." he demonstrated and then asked Randy to feel the corner. Randy deliberately separated the two cards and Carlyle loudly tore him a new a-hole. "You no-good bum, goddamnit, you son-of-a-bitch, what kind of a person feels the corner of a card like that, you ought to be arrested for impersonating a human being...?!"

I shouted out, "He was just yanking your chain, don't drive yourself crazy, it was a joke!" To his credit, Francis instantly looked pretty embarrassed, then exploded with laughter and said, "I was kidding too, just remember, I'm not always right, but I'm never wrong!" It was a quick-witted response; the rest of us cracked up at his mood swing and joke. The fact is, Carlyle was hilarious, a sweetheart, and a very talented artist, who used to drink a little. Actually he used to drink a lot.

When sober, he was an inspiring expert at sleight of hand. When drunk, his funny personality made up for his sloppy manipulations; either way audiences loved him. At one point the Castle cut him off and refused to serve him, but it didn't matter—he would quench his thirst with a swig from a flask he carried in the inside breast pocket of his coat. I was about sixteen, with Francis in the tiny dressing room behind the

Close-up Gallery, when he sneakily slipped his whisky out, touched it to his lips, peeked back, and offered me a sip. "It ain't water," he said, grinning.

At an appointed time, I showed up at Carlyle's apartment so he could teach me a version of a complex card manipulation, the diagonal palm shift. When I got there he was inebriated, but still willing to instruct me. As he handled the cards, his glasses were the perfect barometer of how close he was to passing out. The sleepier he became, the farther down his nose the spectacles would travel.

I watched these descending glasses, and when they reached the tip of his nose, I would prod Francis. Then he would awaken with a little exclamation, adjust the spectacles, repeat the card sleight expressing a pointer or two, until the glasses once again commenced to slide and his voice dissolved into a loud snore. Then, when even my elbow failed to rouse him for perhaps the sixth time, it occurred to me that I had a felt tip marker in my pocket and that it would be funny to draw a little mustache or goatee on his face. But when he awoke I knew he wouldn't take that well, so instead, I just tiptoed out.

Albert Goshman—He had been a bagel baker in Brooklyn, clearly a natural stepping-stone to being a magician, a demonstration of Darwin's law of evolution in reverse. Albert was delightful, lovable, engaging, and looked like a giant dumpling with an oversized bobble head. The face on that head seemed as if it only exhaled, and never inhaled. He had sad, droopy eyes, a large nose, and a big, bushy mustache with waxed ends. He spoke with a lilting, cute, and funny Middle European Yiddish accent, which he exaggerated when performing. "Vahhtt's your name?" Goshman would say to a woman, "I'm going to 'magish' for you." He came in like a lamb but went out like a lion.

He called his presentations "Magic By Gosh" and his Close-up Gallery show, more than anyone else's ever, was a cohesive theatrical beginning, middle, and end experience, complete with a musical score that emanated from a cassette tape player under the table that was operated by Albert's foot. Goshman was arguably the most popular Magic Castle magician in his day. Probably nobody, before or since, has ever come close.

I first met Albert, not at the Castle, but in the men's restroom of The Sportsman's Lodge, in Studio City. As an obsessive magic nut, I recognized him immediately. Albert was about forty-five years old. I was thirteen. We were in the restroom for different reasons, but at the hotel's ballroom for the same reason—Eddie Shlepper's bar mitzvah reception. Well, not the same reason—I was a guest, and Albert was there in a professional capacity as entertainer. Of the two magicians in the restroom, I was the only one there to do number two. Albert was there with a wet paper towel dabbing what appeared to be a food stain on the front of his ruffled tux shirt.

Albert's tabletop production had two human costars, women volunteers, who sat on either side of him. He also had two inanimate co-stars—a salt shaker, which was on the table in front of one of the women, and a pepper shaker in front of the other. As the music came up, the show got underway.

Goshman pulled a couple half-dollars from an invisible purse and asked each woman to say "Go." They did, and the coins vanished, as Albert said "Gone." He glanced at the shakers and asked the women to say "Please." They did, and when they lifted the shakers, the vanished coins were underneath. The coins vanished again, Albert glanced at the shakers, the women picked them up, but there were no coins. "You forgot to say please." The women said "Please." This time when they lifted the shakers, the coins were there. This opening sequence foreshadowed some of the highlights that followed.

Exotic Middle Eastern music played when Albert took out an ornate jewelry box. He shook the box, and verbally imitated the sound, "... *chinka chink, chinka chink*." Then he dumped the contents onto the table, four bottle caps. "Vahhtt? You ver expecting rubies?" The caps were arranged on the table in a square, about a foot apart. Goshman placed each hand over a cap and wiggled his fingers. The caps danced, appeared, and disappeared, in an amazing fashion, eventually assembling one at a time under a single hand. Then they vanished again, and appeared under the shakers.

Albert popularized magic with sponge balls, not only by performing them expertly, but also by manufacturing them and selling them worldwide. His sponge ball company eventually became one of the most financially successful manufacturing businesses in the field of magic tricks, was carried on by his family, and still flourishes as a dominant force today.

He used pale yellow sponge balls in his act, referred to as matzo balls that appeared and disappeared in the women's hands, and seemingly transposed themselves under a bowl. Had the balls transformed into a bagel, or had they disappeared and a bagel appeared in their place? That must have been it, because the balls were found wedged under the shakers.

My favorite of his tricks was when he made a huge coin vanish like magic. In unison the women said "Please," prompting it to reappear under a shaker. It was one thing to have missed the trick with half-dollars, sponge balls, or bottle caps, but this happened, just inches from their eyes, and that coin was the size of a dinner plate! I know, it flabbergasted me with openmouthed astonishment! And I wondered then, as I do now, how he could get away with such an audacious bit of trickery? How I envied him! How I still do!

In 1973, five years after our initial meeting, I was booked to do my close-up act and a lecture at two magic conventions, the Pacific Coast Association of Magicians in Hawaii and Tannen's Jubilee in New York. My expenses were covered, but unfortunately recognition, adulation, and money don't always come together. My show and lecture were received well, but the applause was not bankable. The way magician's magicians make money at a magic convention is to have a ton of stuff that all the attendees want to buy. I was ill-equipped in that department. As I bowed to the clapping, I thought to myself, *If each of you would just throw me a few dollars, I could get my car fixed.*

The headlining all-star performer at both conclaves, who made a bazillion dollars selling the then newly manufactured sponge balls of every size and color to all his fans, was none other than Albert Goshman. At the Jubilee, each evening I sat next to him at our prefix dinner. That's when spaghetti changed my life. It wasn't the spaghetti itself—I'd had better—but it was more meaningful than the chop suey we'd had the night before because of the conversation surrounding the spaghetti.

When he sat down to a meal Goshman appeared as if he felt surrounded by enemies who would snatch his food if he didn't gobble it up first. He clutched his fork and knife as if they were weapons. It was Italian night and Albert speared two meatballs with his fork, the other hand squeezed a sausage and a chunk of bread, half a cannoli smeared his wrist, and strands of spaghetti curled around his tie. But what was most important was his wise-sounding advice.

Hanging around the Castle in those years, I learned that magic was a brutally competitive profession, and there were very few jobs to go around. Sure you pal around with the guys. But according to Goshman, most magicians kept their big important business ideas to themselves. It was rare to meet someone like Goshman who was willing to share secrets that had nothing to do with how to do magic tricks.

I was eighteen, living in a tiny no bedroom dump of an apartment with a couple of roommates. I felt old enough to support myself, but it wasn't easy, and I hated taking even the smallest amount of money from my parents. Besides doing a few of these fraternity of magicians-type events, I was doing magic in rock clubs and also worked at Pants Galore, but I was still having a very tough time making ends meet. Goshman knew how to make money and kindly gave me several tips.

"When you quote $150 and the guy on the other end of the phone offers $100, stick to $150, say, 'I need the money more than you do.' That works most of the time. If it doesn't work, lower your price. You're never worth more than the money you can get. Get the money, get the job."

"If a potential client is on the fence, it's sometimes helpful to tell them you need a decision because you've got five other offers," Albert said, "...even if it's a slight exaggeration, and you have no other offers."

"Charge an extra fee per half hour for wait time. You will book gigs with a start time at ten; you don't go on until eleven, get paid extra for that."

"On outta town gigs always demand first class travel, exchange the airline ticket they provide for an economy seat, and pocket the difference."

"Right now, the best-pay gigs for magicians are in a brand new field, and the good news is, it's wide open, the surface has barely been scratched. Trade shows."

I got a chill. Same then as now, very few earn a living as magicians. It was reminiscent to me of the scene in *The Graduate* where the guy tells Dustin Hoffman to get into the plastics industry, because it's the wave of the future. Unlike Dusty, I was paying close attention. "What's a trade show?"

"A trade show is an exhibition where companies in a specific industry promote their products and services. I just did the auto show for Champion spark plugs, got a biz machine deal coming up for IBM."

"What do you do?"

"Every company has a booth. I do shows in front of my sponsor's booth. The magic attracts a crowd. To get people interested in the company, I deliver a marketing message as part of my act. It's like an in-person TV commercial. And I do it over and over and over, eight to ten hours a day."

"Eight to ten hours a day?"

"I drink quarts of black coffee and perspire like a pig. But I don't get those soaking discolored rings of sweat you'd expect to see under my arms; I got a trick for that. Kind of a trade show, trade secret..."

"Yeah, okay, what's the secret?"

"Under my shirt, under each arm, I tape an absorbing sanitary napkin panty pad."

MY FIRST "HAND JOB"

I gave my first "hand job" at the age of fourteen. I did it for the man from Glad. When I say Glad, I'm not talking about Gays & Lesbians Against Defamation. I'm talking about the company that makes plastic sandwich and garbage bags.

Back in the day, there was a TV commercial for Glad sandwich bags that featured a guy known as the Man from Glad. He was dressed in white pants, a white shirt, white jacket, white shoes, white socks, and probably underwear that's white and fresh and soft as newly fallen snow. At one point he demonstrated how to close the sandwich bag. You'd see a close-up of white gloved hands demonstrating, and hear the words, "... fold this flap in, and this flap over ... that's all there is to it."

The guy doing the "hand job," or if you prefer "body double" work, as the white gloved hands, was Leo Behnke. When I was growing up Leo was a popular magician at the Magic Castle and had gained a reputation doing "hand jobs" for Glad television commercials.

On screen, he made those sandwich bags look easy to close in two seconds. Sounds simple, but the flap-folding system was an acquired knack, unlike the simple zip lock concept that eventually evolved.

When Glad started manufacturing garbage bags, one of their first commercials featured a boy raking leaves. Leo Behnke arranged auditions to cast a pair of boy's hands for the close-ups, and he's the one who put me in front of the producers, and ultimately the guy who got me the job. I got my first "hand job" from a Magic Castle magician!

Not unlike the funky flap-folding system that preceded the zip-lock sandwich bags, before the simple twist ties used to close garbage bags came along, Glad had a crazy little device to do the job. It was a sliver of plastic, one end was jagged, the other end had a slot cut in it, and to close the bag, you'd wrap the plastic sliver around the top of the garbage bag then pull the jagged end through the slot.

If you were in the waiting room at the audition, you would have seen some frustrated teenage boys attempting to operate these plastic slivers on foam-filled garbage bags. To make a long story short or a short story long, I got the gig.

Even though only my hands would be seen in the commercial, and nobody in the world would know they were my hands, and they'd only be on screen for a fraction of an instant, I was still very excited. The day before the shoot I was thinking about what interpretation I could bring to my part.

The commercial was shot on the front lawn of a nice house on a tree-lined street. The freckled teen actor with red hair looked perfectly natural raking leaves. In another shot he held the sides of the garbage bag while his foot stomped inside, making room for more leaves and effectively demonstrating the rugged durability of the Glad product.

They'd been shooting over six hours before my turn came. My years of sleight-of-hand training were about to be put into practice. I needed to be calm, I needed to be focused, and I needed to remember to breathe. Finally the shot was done. We did it in three takes, for a total of about five minutes, but it took the life experience of a boy magician to make my first onscreen starring role look easy.

DR. Q's
HYPNOTIC ACT

One afternoon I was in the Magic Castle library, flipping through a stack of books, when Bill Larsen poked his head in.

"Can I be of some assistance?"

"Next week I'm doing a Cub Scout show and I need a new trick idea. Something really big ... something that I can close the show with ... something in one of these books ... something that doesn't cost any money. What can I do?" Bill had the answer.

The year was 1969, and I was almost fifteen years old. Outside of the one twenty-minute show a week I was doing for free at the Castle on Sunday nights, this was one of my very first professional gigs. I was offered seven dollars, which also made it one of my very first well-paying jobs.

An audience of seventy-five people, a much larger group than I was used to in the Close-up Gallery, was expected to attend the annual Cub Scout Blue & Gold Banquet at Shakey's Pizza Parlor. I'd seen the piano and banjo duo that entertained regularly at this particular Shakey's, so I knew what to expect. No stage and a very close audience on three sides surrounding the performance space in front of the piano.

Bill said the answer was in a manuscript written by his father, William Larsen, Sr., in 1944, *Dr. Q's Hypnotic Act*. Not real hypnotism, but a routine that looked like it to the audience. Best of all, there were no secret assistants, no prearrangements, and no apparatus or props needed. I could present this celebrated act and give the Cub Scouts a hypnotic exhibition. Or could I? Here now are the first two paragraphs of the manuscript.

"Thayer's Studio of Magic is pleased to be able to offer the magic fraternity, Dr. Q's own Hypnotic Act—together with his inimitable method of presentation.

"We wish first to warn the reader not to let the extreme simplicity of Dr. Q's unique hypnotic methods scare you from using this sensational act. Give it a try on your very next show, and we feel sure you will keep it in the act ever after. Dr. Q's Hypnotic Act has been successfully performed before every type of audience...its daring audacity being the key to its very brilliance."

What followed was the inimitable presentation, which started with a two-page monologue describing the many then-current articles (in 1944) appearing about this phenomenon called hypnosis that was sweeping the country, and how the best hypnotic subjects were persons with very high intelligence. The script was conceived to sell the audience almost instantly on the fact that you knew your subject, and interest them intently in what you were about to do. Also, it placed the volunteers at ease about participating, removed them from any later criticism, and made them feel smart and eager to cooperate.

"Science has proven that only the most intelligent and creative people respond to hypnosis, and those who participate in my demonstration will be treated with the utmost in courtesy and respect. And now, without further ado, I wish to invite several of you gentlemen up on this stage to participate in these demonstrations in hypnotism. Will five gentlemen please step forward? Thank you, sirs."

I carefully read the manuscript, thought about it, loved it, but saw problems for me to overcome in order to do it at the scout show. First, the opening monologue of the script was two pages of stuff that just did not sound like it could come out of my mouth. At least that problem, I thought, I could deal with. But the Dr. Q hypnotic method was a complete fakeroo that didn't seem suited to my circumstance.

The manuscript said to have five volunteers stand on the stage in a row about two feet apart. And under cover of the sound of the orchestra playing, the magician was to stand in front of the volunteer on the left end of the line, turn his back to the audience, and make mystical gestures in front of his face, while saying, "We are going to have a good laugh on the audience and fool them, so when I tell you to do some funny things, do exactly as I say. Okay? Swell!" Then it said to go down the line repeating this to each volunteer.

Well, that was also a problem. There was no sound system for this gig—not even a microphone, or a turntable or eight-track player to cover the sound of the secret talk. And there was no stage. The audience would be close and surrounding the performance. I'd be busted even if I whispered the secret instructions to a volunteer. Plus I felt five would be too many volunteers to manage at one time.

Still, I wanted to make this fake hypnosis demonstration work, and I did.

Cut to my hypnosis demonstration at the annual Cub Scout Blue & Gold Banquet, in front of the piano at Shakey's Pizza Parlor in 1969.

"Recently I had the pleasure of seeing the great Dr. Q's hypnosis show and I wanted to share what it was like if you were sitting next to me in the front row," I announced. "I'm going to need three cubs to hypnotize. If you are extremely intelligent, have a big imagination, and can focus enough to cooperate with me, please raise your hand now."

I picked Robert, David, and James as volunteers, and had them stand a few feet apart, facing the audience. I went to the one on the left end of the line, Robert, and faced him, deliberately turning my back on most of the audience, and placed my left hand on the back of his neck, at the base of the brain, and squeezed gently.

According to the manuscript, the psychological effect of this was to render the helper a "willing dupe." The stance, with the pressure upon his neck, put you in a position of dominance. This, coupled with my position as "master of the stage," was supposed to make the helper amenable to do exactly what I told him.

At the same time, my free right hand reached into my right jacket coat pocket and took out a marble and held it in front of him and I said, "Robert, stare into this tiny crystal ball," and I continued saying the sort of stuff you might hear a real hypnotist say—"Robert, your eyelids are getting heavy. Robert, you're getting sleepy. Robert, it's hard to keep your eyes open . . . "

What the audience couldn't see, is that in the hand holding the marble, I also held a small card—secretly holding stuff in your hand is what we magic types call palming—so while Robert was looking at the marble, he was also staring at the card hidden in the palm of my hand. Neatly typed on that palmed business-sized card were written these words:

We are going to have a good laugh on the audience and fool them, so when I tell you to do some funny things, do exactly as I say.

Although my secret message was written, and not spoken as outlined in the manuscript, it was still presented in the form of a confidence of producing laughs on the rest of the spectators in the audience. According to the manuscript, this would make the volunteer feel important that he was in on the secret, and that he was to become "part of the show."

As Robert read the secret message, I boldly said, "Okay, swell," which seemed to imply his automatic willingness to follow my written instructions, and then I winked at him in a friendly way. The wink clinched the spirit of "good fellowship" between us. I handled everything as outlined in the manuscript, which stated . . .

"Handled thus, any spectator that happens to come up on the stage quickly becomes a 'perfect hypnotic subject' for your demonstrations." Dr. Q is certainly to be commended for developing this perfectly brilliant psychological method of "handling" the subjects.

I snapped my fingers, and guess what? Robert closed his eyes and slumped forward. Perfect. If he really were hypnotized, he probably would have done the exact same thing.

I proceeded to David. I took the same stance with him, showed him the palmed secret message under the guise of having him stare at the marble in my hand, and said the same words as I had done with Robert. David caught on even quicker than Robert; before I even snapped my fingers he shut his eyes, allowed his arms to dangle, and tilted his head to one side.

To the audience, it looked like I had hypnotized these cubs, and since that's what they were expecting me to do, it all passed naturally. They saw my stern position as I gazed into the eyes of the boys who were focused on the marble, and even the fact that David's lips moved while he read the secret note—that mumbling seemed to add to the expected "hypnotic formula" used in hypnotizing.

Then came James. I did my thing, but he just stood there with his arms crossed across his chest in a defiant sort of pose. He wasn't willing to get with the program. We just stared at one another, as if we were both stunned for a moment. I snapped out of it, put the marble and hidden message back in my pocket, left James standing there with his arms folded, and went back to my first helper Robert.

"Robert, in a moment I'm going to count to three. When you hear the number three, I'm going to snap my fingers. When I snap, you will open your eyes and become a world famous rodeo champion. Next to you is a piano bench; when I snap my fingers that piano bench will look like a wild bucking bull. Jump on that bull and ride 'em cowboy! Show us what you're made of!"

On my command Robert hopped on the piano bench, bounced up and down, waved his hand in the air, and the entire scout troop was in hysterics. "Robert, when I clap my hands, you will go back into a deep hypnotic sleep," when I did, he suddenly went limp, and I stepped in front of David. James was still standing on the end with his arms folded and his eyes wide open in a defiant pose.

"David, in a moment I'm going to count to three. When you hear the number three, I'm going to snap my fingers. When I snap, you will be a fisherman. I want you to cast your reel and catch a big one, struggle with the fish, and then I want you to dive in and swim." On my command David obeyed and again the cubs were wild with laughter. "David, when I clap my hands, you will go back into a deep hypnotic sleep." I did and he did.

Before I could say another word, my third volunteer, James, shouted, "You're not going to make a monkey out of me!" There were a few snickers and giggles; then the entire crowd started chanting, "James! James! James! James! James..."

I did some quick thinking. With all the noise from the hollered chanting, no one but James could hear me, "James, just play along and I'll give you a dollar." I put a hand over my heart and two fingers in the air, "Scouts honor." All of a sudden he was docile, and willing to follow my instructions. At the top of my lungs I screamed, "James you are a monkey!"

James hunched over, jumped up and down, scratched under his arms, loudly grunted chimp noises, and the audience roared with laughter. Then I shouted loudly, "Sleep," and he dropped to the floor in a heap.

Before I go any further, it would be prudent to point out the value of a dollar in 1969. It was a lot of money for a boy in that long-ago time. At the Shakey's banquet the ticket cost a single dollar per person, and included pizza, salad, soda, and a scoop of ice cream.

By this time, so much attention had been heaped on the boys, and the audience was laughing so loudly. My volunteers had so caught on to what was expected of them and were having such a swell time making the audience laugh, that they probably would have done anything I suggested at the slightest provocation.

Bluntly speaking, at this point the cubs and I were co-conspirators, and certainly felt they were in on the scam. The manuscript suggested finishing with some post-hypnotic suggestions, specified actions to be performed after the cubs awakened from their deep hypnotic trances.

"I'd like to thank each of you for volunteering to help with the demonstrations. When I clap my hands, you will awaken. Robert, when you awaken I want you to beat your chest and holler like Tarzan. David, give a quick acceptance speech for the best actor 1969 Oscar you just won. James, you will be convinced I owe you money. It all happens now, when I clap my hands..."

Robert beat his chest and gave a Tarzan holler. David said he'd like to thank his parents for making it all possible. James looked at me and screamed, "You owe me a dollar!" When I sent the Cubs back to their seats they got a crazy humongous ovation. "Young man," the Scoutmaster said, breaking into a smile, "I liked what I saw tonight, and I want you to perform at my Rotary Club meeting." Wow! Ka-Ching! Another seven dollars!

Between that night and the Rotary Club, the Scoutmaster told his buddies I could hypnotize anyone. "Not me," said a fellow Rotarian named Bernard. Unbeknownst to me a bottle of scotch was bet, riding on my ability to hypnotize the skeptic. Turns out the Rotary Club met at the same Shakey's. As I was having my three selected Rotarian volunteers join me in front of the piano, a fourth Rotarian who I didn't select also stepped up—Bernard.

Not knowing about the bet, I assumed Bernard to be a willing participant, and accepted him as an extra helper ready to have some fun.

When I asked Bernard to stare at the marble, he grabbed the hidden palmed card with the neatly typed secret message out of my hand, and ran to show it to the Scoutmaster. Bernard won his bottle of scotch. Fortunately the Scoutmaster seemed only slightly annoyed that his wager had gone sour. He told me I'd shown everyone a good time, and that's what really counted, even if it cost him a little hooch. I was a little ashamed when I sheepishly accepted my seven bucks for the show, but felt that all is well that ends well.

About two weeks after I wrote this chapter, for some nostalgic fun, I made a new secret card, palmed it, and tried Dr. Q's Hypnotic Method for a couple weeks in my Magicopolis show. This time, as an adult with a lot of shows under my belt, I felt comfortable experimenting. I started with a half-dozen subjects, and then, for a finish, trimmed the herd down to the two who to that point gave the very best performances. Whether it was two men, two women, or one of each, the two remaining were the best of the best.

"You two are on your honeymoon...on a desert island. The moon is shinning its magical glow, and you two are deeply, deeply, in love. When I snap my fingers you will awaken from your hypnotic trance, and be in your romantic tropical paradise..."

When I snapped my fingers, it was always a surprise. The funniest was when two men played paddy cake, then exchanged shirts and waltzed together, before I woke them from their trance and sent them back to their seats to a thunderous applause. Not long after, my personal fun with the bit faded and I dumped the hypnosis. Besides the fun aspect, frankly, the bit really wasn't up to the level of the other material in the show.

A couple months later, I got a call from a party planner offering to hire me to perform at a retirement party. The only stipulation was that the act ended with my hypnosis demonstration. No problem, the gig was booked. The big bash was held around the corner from Magicopolis at the Viceroy Hotel. Upon my arrival, the party planner gave me a list of names she wanted to assist me with the hypnosis demonstration. I started to explain how the spontaneous selection of volunteers worked best for me, but she was insistent, and demanded that the two names circled in red be the honeymooners, so naturally, I said "no worries," and that was that.

There was the usual buffet, drinks, etc. When it came time to do the show, the retiree whom the soiree was thrown for, a career radio exec, introduced me with a big buildup.

I walked out a bit nervously; for some reason the audience seemed like it might be a tough one, but very sharp. I relaxed quickly and after I did my stuff, I got an ovation!

The crowd kept applauding and shouting, "more, more," which was great since I still hadn't done the hypnosis, but also not so great, since I felt the hypnosis was my weakest material. Nevertheless, I forged ahead, right down to the last two hypnotic volunteers, two extraordinarily beautiful girls. One looked like a Victoria's Secret model, the other like a *Playboy* centerfold.

"You two are on your honeymoon . . . on a deserted desert island . . ."

In a fraction of an instant both girls were totally naked and engaged in full-on super-hot lesbian lovemaking. The crowd went wild out of control, and suddenly there were naked girls everywhere. I guess that party planner knew what she was doing.

WORLD'S GREATEST MAGICIANS AT THE MAGIC CASTLE

Chronologically speaking, this chapter is out of order, but I'm including it here so it will be closer to my Magic Castle era stuff. The title above was the title of a CBS TV special that was broadcast in September 1990. It's easy for me to jump ahead seventeen years from 1973 in this book, but in real life I don't want to jump ahead ten seconds...what am I talking about, make that five. Anyway, the host was a magic fan, Peter Scolari, who was/is best known for his roles in the television shows *Newhart, Honey, I Shrunk the Kids: The TV Show,* and *Bosom Buddies,* the last of which he co-starred in with a then-little-known Tom Hanks.

As the title implies, the location was the Magic Castle and the show featured a who's who of top-notch late eighties magicians performing illusions and close-up magic. A guy with dark sunglasses and a goose was also in the cast. I was the guy with the goose. The program was filmed between 3:00 a.m. and 3:00 p.m. to avoid the Castle's normal operating ours. My call time was 4:30 a.m.

Upon arrival I was directed to the parking lot, where I found my very own trailer dressing room. I unloaded my stuff and had a look around. The lights worked, the toilet flushed, and there was even hot water, real flowers, and a basket of fruit. Next stop, the brightly lit makeup and hair trailer. My face was their business and they had a big job disguising my every wart, scar, and blemish. I slept through the glamour treatment. Drooling was an issue and I was told I snored. Between arrival and makeup, two and a half hours had elapsed.

At 7:00 a.m. I emerged from my trailer wearing dark sunglasses and an electric-blue silk suit, and held under my arm was a life-size stuffed animal puppet goose. At 7:15 a.m. I was in my performance space, the Parlor of Prestidigitation, and someone shouted "Okay, here we go!" The crew went through its pre-take gyrations, "All right—three, two, one, action!"

"This is Geyser, the world's only clairvoyant goose. He's a mind reader...he's gonna be reading some minds and I'm here to prove it to you." I pointed to someone in the audience, "What's your name?" It looked like the goose whispered in my ear, and I said, "The goose knew that...don't worry, it gets better."

Hey, which one do you think is me?

"I'd like you to please think of any number from one to ten. Concentrate...the goose is getting an impression..." I put a felt tip marker in the goose's beak, and the goose wrote a number on a pad of paper. No one could see what number he'd written. "The goose has made his decision. Tell everyone, what number were you thinking of? Nine? Excellent, if the goose got it, he'll expect thunderous applause to ensue."

I turned around the pad of paper and sure enough, written in bold magic marker was the number nine. "Not bad for a goose."

"We're going to take this a step further. If you would, Sir, please point to some woman in the audience, someone that you don't know. I think he means you Madam. If you would, please, think of any letter in the alphabet. The goose is going to read your mind. Concentrate. The goose is getting an impression."

Suddenly, the goose let loose with an unexpected stream of urine. "Oh gee whizz. He's just a goose. He doesn't know any better. Were you thinking of the letter P? Of course you were. That explains it. Good the first fella didn't think number two.

"Now, if you would, Miss, please point to a fella, someone you don't know, we're going to take this a step further..."

I asked the guy picked, "Do you have any change in your pocket? Excellent. Concentrate on the amount you have. Time for some high powered mind reading now." I put shades on the goose that matched the ones I was wearing. Instantly the stuffed animal got an impression and wrote a number. "The goose has made his decision. How much change you got there? Thirty-six cents? Take a look." Sure enough, the goose had written thirty-six cents. "Not bad for a goose!"

At the director's request I ran through the routine twice more, interacting with new audience members each time, each time changing up the dialogue with ad-libs and various bits in the goose's repertoire. Next the director turned his attention to the audience.

To sell the idea that the Castle was filled with real people being entertained—normally not the case between 3:00 a.m. and 3:00 p.m.—the production had employed an audience of extras. You know all of those people you see wandering around the background of your favorite movies and television shows—those are extras. These particular extras were provided with white tie and tails, tuxedos, long elegant gowns, and professional hair and makeup. At a glance, they looked like opening night opera attendees.

Extras aren't always professional actors, or they are actors who probably wouldn't ever make it. In fact, most extras are just regular folk who want to be a part of the film and television industry. When they assisted me and my goose they weren't on camera and they seemed somewhat natural and unrehearsed.

That all changed when the camera was pointed at them, they were miked, in the spotlight, and asked to reenact their comments and reactions. Fake laughs, exaggerated expressions, and simple answers like, "yeah" became sentences like "Yes. That. Is. Correct. Sir. Ha. Ha. Ha."

Kind of a catch-22. I understood the necessity of the spectator shots—otherwise my routine might look like half of a phone conversation. On the other hand, when costumed camera-aware extras reenact their comments and reactions to a magician—and it looks fake and/or rehearsed—it can be jarring to home viewers and make the extras look more like shills than a real audience.

Watching the special at home I was impressed to see how all the shots from three different performances and nine or ten different audience members were boiled down and cobbled together into a coherent whole that looked live and unedited.

But I was disappointed. It seemed to me that the funniest audience by-play and ad libs were missing, and most disappointing, the entire pee sequence had vanished. I, like all immature adults, thought that pee bit was funny. As far as I was concerned, my goose had been flambéed.

Not long after the show aired, its producer, Troy Miller, hired me as a magic consultant for a short film called *Dr. Goldfarb, Physician-Magician*, which was a show within a show broadcast on the then-young FOX network. Being on set gave me the opportunity to ask Mr. Miller what happened to the pee. He told me that the network approved all programming and the cut was made because it was a violation of a thing called CBS standards and practices.

Amongst the magic I consulted on the FOX show was a shot of the physician-magician pulling a string of credit cards from a patient's posterior. So I casually asked Mr. Miller how that could air but pee couldn't? He answered honestly saying that the big idea at the FOX network was to air content you could normally only see on cable.

Recently I saw part of a sitcom on CBS. In 1990 CBS was CBS. It didn't look like FOX, which looks like ABC, which you can't tell apart from NBC like today. This is a new and brighter world. I'm certain, nowadays, were a goose to pee on broadcast or cable, it would be rerun five times in slow motion and celebrated.

I have fond memories of doing that Magic Castle TV special and it helped me out many years later. Without my advance knowledge or permission, in 2008 a guy in merry old England produced an instructional DVD featuring the Mind-reading Goose. The fact that I had done it on television back in 1990 established a definitive copyright for my routine.

The producer of the offending DVD was informed that if he were sued for copyright infringement and didn't come from the UK to defend himself in a Los Angeles court, he'd lose the case by default. The consequence being that a lien would be put on his passport, preventing him from entering the USA without first resolving the dispute. Said producer claimed to be unaware his artist was unauthorized to perform the bit; having been informed, he graciously recalled the DVDs and issued a sincere and heartfelt apology.

Not the usual outcome when dealing with bootlegging pirates, even unknowing ones. Throughout magic's first million years there has been a ton of intellectual theft, but I know of only two controversies where the injured party prevailed by legal means. My buddy Teller won a lawsuit against a Belgian who copycatted his poetic and stunning Shadows trick, and David Copperfield's lawsuit against a French magician who copied his flying routine. Lovely anecdotes with which to end this chapter, don't cha think?

CARTER'S MAGIC CELLAR

Back to 1973, the one place on the face of the earth outside of the Magic Castle or a magic convention, that afforded me the opportunity to do a formal close-up show on a regular basis, was in the basement of a jazz club in San Francisco by the name of Earthquake McGoon's. The story of the basement and how it became a venue for magic goes like this . . .

A musician named Turk Murphy owned and appeared nightly with his jazz band at Earthquake McGoon's on Clay Street. Turk and his partner shared a warehouse with the nephew of a famous Roaring Twenties era illusionist know as Carter the Great. One day the old brick warehouse was condemned by the city and ordered demolished.

In the warehouse, Murphy and his partner stored foreign classic cars, which they imported for fun and profit. Next to the cars, Carter's nephew stored his Uncle Charlie's magic show in fifty-one old theatrical trunks. The nephew couldn't, or didn't want to, find a new home for the trunks and they ended up with Murphy.

The unused basement of Earthquake McGoon's was decorated with the contents of the trunks, Carter the Great posters, vintage illusions, props, and costumes. Carter's Magic Cellar opened on the weekends starting in 1972, and beginning the following year, one Saturday night a month, I performed my close-up show there.

I would have gladly performed in the Cellar every Saturday night, but I couldn't afford it. I was paid $25 a night, out of which I had to pay for gas to make the 800-mile round trip drive from LA to San Francisco, a room at the YMCA, food, gratuities, and city, state, and federal taxes (Okay, truth be told, I never paid the taxes. Hope the statute of limitations is up on that). With penalties and interest accrued since 1973 that could add up to a pretty penny, and counting.

My name was hand-printed with a marker on an index card at the top of the stairs that led down to the Cellar. The audiences came from the jazz club upstairs; they would filter down to our basement location during the band breaks. Although I did many of the same tricks at the Cellar that I did in the Close-up Gallery at the Magic Castle, the audiences here were closer to the ones I encountered doing my stand-up in the Hollywood rock clubs, and I adjusted my San Francisco presentations accordingly.

When I opened the box, as I took out my deck of cards, a joint fell onto the table. Sometimes a member of the crowd grabbed for it; either way, the joint flew back into my hand. The bit was a fun opener and always got me off to a great start. I did it with what magicians call a reel, also sometimes sold in gag shops as a Money Snatcher, because it is commonly used with a dollar bill.

The fake joint was secretly taped to the end of a two-foot piece of black silk thread. I held the Dollar Snatcher reel, which was about the size of four stacked quarters, in the same hand that held the card box, so it was hidden underneath. I accidentally dropped the joint as I took out the cards, pressed the button, and *whap*—the reel quickly pulled the joint to me. It was simple and ridiculous and got laughs.

The Quaalude, a large round flat pill, was a fashionable new designer drug of the day, and head shops—what we used to call stores where you could buy pipes, roach clips, and bongs—sold candy replicas of them. Known also as "Ludes," I used the candy ones in place of coins for my trick, Ludes through Table.

I showed four Quaaludes in one hand, tapped the table top, and immediately, the pills were spread to reveal that only three Ludes were left in what was a stack of four. Showing my other hand empty, I reached beneath the table and brought the missing Quaalude into view—it had apparently "magically" penetrated through the tabletop.

This feat was repeated with the remaining pills, one at a time, until all four Ludes had passed through the table. Before reaching under the table to produce the final one, I said, "Did you see that last Lude go? No? It was big enough." Then I tossed a huge saucer-sized Lude on the table. This trick was particularly impressive to members of the audience that preferred real Quaaludes to the candy ones.

The Gymnastic Aces, a trick that worked well for me at the Castle—as part of a presentation about how different experts from around the world can cut any cards desired from a shuffled deck—was even more of a pleaser at the Cellar when I renamed it the Dick Trick. The cards were examined and shuffled by a guy I'll call Dave.

I said, "Dave, we're going to pretend this deck is your baby maker." I shuffled the cards by repeatedly drawing cards off the top, from the ends of the deck, the shorter sides of the cards, instead of drawing them sideways as with the overhand shuffle. It's called the Hindu Shuffle, supposedly named after Hindu magicians who were unfamiliar with the usual shuffling methods. Whatever its origin, it looked exactly like I was masturbating the deck.

I cut the cards in half and weaved the short ends together so the deck looked twice as long as it normally did. "Oh, wait Dave, this is supposed to be your flesh flute." I pushed the cards together slightly, making the length of the deck a little shorter. "Dave, I see you're getting excited." I started to shake the deck. "The moment of ecstasy is close . . ." Suddenly all the aces ejaculated out the end of the deck. Yes, I was very proud of my close-up show at Carter's Magic Cellar.

PART FOUR

FUNNY BUSINESS

COMEDY CLUBS

Shortly before I moved to Aspen, the Magic Castle completed a remodel job that included the addition of a hundred-seat showroom, named the Palace of Mystery. My Los Angeles vacations to visit family and friends always included a one-week engagement in the Palace. On a 1978 visit, the talent coordinator from the newly opened Comedy & Magic Club in Hermosa Beach was in the Castle audience. Thereafter, I was also booked in Hermosa for weekly gigs when in town.

From the start, among the things that made Hermosa unique was that it featured magicians with comedians, another being that the location catered to very responsive audiences as opposed to the more jaded industry types one might encounter at Hollywood's Improv or Comedy Store. Perfecto, plus there was pay and free eats. At Hermosa gigs, I appeared with and admired the talent of consummate pros such as Jay Leno, Jerry Seinfeld, and Garry Shandling, before they hit it big. Actually, I think Jay Leno still appears there on Sunday nights.

By the time I moved back to LA in 1985, comedy clubs had popped up. It seemed that a brick wall and a microphone were available everywhere. As a result of Hermosa being my home club, bookings materialized for me at other local venues like the Ice House, LA Comedy Club, and Igby's, as well as comedy spots throughout the USA and Canada.

The great thing about comedy clubs, not unlike the Jester in Aspen, and unlike practically all other gigs, was that they were a safe haven to develop new material. They were places you could experiment with untried and untrue bits between your sure-fire opening and closing, something you could never risk performing at casinos, dinner theaters, or corporate events. It was not unlike the rock club process when I developed the Highdini act.

Winning a comedy club audience right away was important. As a magician it was essential to have a great opening to establish the funny, yet differentiate myself from straight stand-ups. A number of them were tried before settling on a keeper that established what I was going for and was a crowd pleaser.

The cliché symbol of a magician is the rabbit in the hat. I held up an empty hat, and there was an explosion. Boom! The flames burst up in an orange ball of fire and a cloud of black smoke erupted from the topper. The smoke cleared, and out popped a skeletal, smoldering, blown-apart bunny. "It's not a real bunny rabbit, but it used to be." Now that was my idea, at the time, of comedy magic.

Have explosives, will travel.

116

Hidden in the hat was a flash pot, a device consisting of a short, open-ended lead pipe stuffed with gunpowder that was ignited with a battery operated switch. I traveled thousands of miles across the USA and around the world to make people laugh with that bomb. It was completely illegitimate, but I felt it was far better to plead for forgiveness than to ask for permission, and never once did I have to ask for forgiveness. Keep in mind, this was long before 9/11, and airport security wasn't what it is today. Now, just to perform that trick on stage, legally, would require a permit, a fireman, and a licensed pyrotechnic expert.

The closing was just as important as the opening, and I often finished with my version of the classic East Indian Needle Mystery. I would appear to swallow twenty to thirty sewing needles and three feet of thread, and bring the needles up threaded. At the time, this was an obscure outdated unseen sideshow stunt I'd resurrected with a humorous slant. A few highlights:

A volunteer was handed a flashlight. I opened my mouth and had him take a look down my throat.

"What do you see?"

"Nothing."

"Last night the guy said hemorrhoids. I was surprised he could see that far."

The helper inspected a number of stainless steel sewing needles. Each needle was nearly three inches in length. He handed them to me one at a time, and watched me swallow them. To insure I wasn't hiding any needles in my mouth, after each swallow, aided by the flashlight, he looked inside my mouth, under my tongue, the top gum, bottom gum, and the sides of my mouth.

The situation and jokes built until a bunch of needles had been swallowed along with some thread. I claimed the thread was "a little al dente," and at this point I reiterated that "all the needles and the thread had passed to the stomach through the fallopian tube." As the volunteer did his duty, at my request, the entire audience loudly chanted his directives.

"Inside the mouth! Under the tongue! The top gum! Bottom gum! Sides of the mouth!"

"Who said the nose? Don't make me laugh—I'll tack you to the wall. Actually I went in for a nose job; they told me it would be cheaper to make my face bigger. Oh good, you're smiling now. If you suppress your laughter it comes out the other end."

The volunteer stood to my right and his left hand held the flashlight pointed toward my mouth. I had him put his right hand on his waist and asked him, "Do you know the song 'I'm a Little Teapot'?"

For the finish I had the audience do a drum roll on their tabletops and brought up the threaded needles to thunderous applause.

On the road, club owners and their audiences loved the rare funny magician, juggler, ventriloquist, or musical act that brought variety to shows. Some stand-ups, however, were not so welcoming to performers who used props, dummies, guitars, or gadgets, even if they were other comedians. More than once I got the cold shoulder from pure monologists who felt that appearing onstage with anything more than a microphone was not to be tolerated in a comedy club.

The guy who got the most heat by far was Gallagher, who had an eleven-foot pole for people you wouldn't touch with a ten-foot pole, glasses with windshield wipers to be worn when eating grapefruit, and whose Sledge-o-matic routine was very popular with audiences in the 1980s. The more successful Gallagher became, the more certain comics ridiculed him.

Ofttimes I'd have a revenge of sorts on the purists when my laughs and ovations hit a level that were hard to follow, and club owners would swap me from feature to headline status. Revenge can be sweet, but a headliner demoted to the middle of the show was not generally a happy camper who instantly became my fan or friend.

On the other hand, if you are a headliner and you get a mediocre response, compared to to the act right before you, who absolutely kills, it doesn't feel so good. Perhaps not a brutal beating, but more like a swift slap to the ego. That happened to me in Arizona where my shows as the headliner were a comfortable cruise at The Comedy Boat in Phoenix, until political satirist Will Durst dropped in to do an unexpected guest spot.

The native San Franciscan was in town to soak up the sun and watch the baseball Giants go through their spring training paces. Will was a Giants fan and the Giants and company were Will fans who packed the club that night, laughing and cheering their man to a decisive comedy victory over yours truly. Following him on stage was a nightmare. I was desperately hoping there would be a disaster that would put an end to my agony and clear the club. Nothing malicious or arrogant about Will Durst—he didn't murder me deliberately, of course. The audience just liked him better than me.

When a show went well I felt completely exhilarated, but if I'd just finished a show I wasn't happy with, like the one where I followed Will Durst, I would console myself by imagining the sound of a cash register ringing. At least for a little while I could rationalize my unhappiness away with the fact that the pay was okay. But, of course, I liked it the other way, when the show worked well, the audience liked it, and I felt I'd done my best work.

The majority of comics I worked with were gracious, supportive, and good company. As a rule, accommodations were generally in economy motel rooms or apartments, called comedy condos, where road acts roomed together. Living and breathing the same rarified offstage air as some of these talented professional funny men often gave me an insight into their unique characters.

Bill Hicks, the bad boy comedy outlaw, was my roommate and co-star in Atlantic City at the Comedy Stop at the Trop for a week. Onstage he was angry, explosive, gleeful, evil, and very funny, with all-knowing grins igniting his face. His

119

words were violent, obscene, wise, astonishing, appalling, liberating, and blasphemous. Offstage in the comedy condo he was a nonstop free association stream-of-consciousness conversationalist; nightly we talked into the wee hours. We crashed at dawn, woke at 5:00 p.m., and that was our breakfast time. I didn't catch up with my body clock until the Atlantic City gig was in my rearview mirror.

One trick I did at the time was disguised to look like mental telepathy. That bit got us talking about metaphysics and the possibility of real telepathy, which I didn't and don't believe in, but which Bill thought he personally experienced on a regular basis.

In my pseudo-psychometry routine, audience members secretly put various personal items such as a watch, lipstick, comb, or lighter, into a bag. Without knowing what belonged to whom, I would reach into the bag, take out an object, get some vibes from it, and tell something about the object's owner, like, "Your birthstone is plastic, you have no future." The magic part was that I returned each object to its correct owner. No real telepathy, a trick pure and simple, and Bill knew that, of course. But that trick was a discussion starter that propelled numerous conversations throughout our week together about Bill's "real" telepathic experiences.

There were a lot of them, but personally, I chalked them all up to coincidence, and told him so. Bill was most impressed by two incidents connected to deaths. One was when his watch stopped at the exact time a distant relative passed away, the other time was when he was staring at a poster of John Lennon on his wall. Then the picture wire broke. The large glass-covered poster fell and almost knocked him unconscious; it was the day Lennon was shot. Bill said he also experienced other sorts of phenomena connected with deaths.

When I brought up the idea of being superstitious, he said he was only superstitious when it came to luck. Actually, despite all the telepathic and psychic phenomena he felt he experienced, what he really said was that he wasn't superstitious at all, but I suspect he had his fingers crossed when he said that. We conversed about aesthetics and technology and music and women, holding opposite views, though I don't know which was Bill's and which was mine, and I think that both of us at times became a little confused about that.

We talked about how magic tricks looked one way when they were really another way. This led to discussions on misdirection outside the realm of the magician. Bill said that magicians' principles of misdirection and trickery might be among the techniques used by governments to manipulate the media and by churches to hide truths from the flock, and that the magic of magicians could be used to accomplish a laundry list of other sociological atrocities. But Bill appreciated the fact that what he considered to be devious methods could be used ethically by a magician to entertain audiences.

Bill entertained me with his guitar and loved watching me perform every card trick I knew. There were no tricks with cards in Bill's repertoire, but watching him cut and shuffle the deck, it was obvious to me he had some inherent manipulative skill. By the end of the week I was able to teach him, and he was able to master several basic sleights. Bill took a lot of notes on how those few sleights could be combined in various ways to perform a number of different baffling tricks. He said it was like knowing a few guitar chords that could be combined to play different songs, and he was right.

The first time I worked with the esoteric deadpan king of one-liners, Steven Wright, a teenage David Spade who was destined for "Saturday Night Live" and sitcom success, was the emcee. We were all at Finney Bones, a Phoenix club owned by comedy magician Michael Finney. What was most surprising is that Steven had just had a hit comedy album, had just done an HBO special, and was about to embark on his first national college tour.

So what was he doing at a tiny club in Phoenix? Working on new material, that's what. This was his laboratory. He was constantly writing jokes, and by his own estimate, only one in ten of his bizarre one-liners was a winner. Steven would read joke after joke off his lined yellow pad of paper, and if the audience didn't respond, he'd cross the joke off the list. His slow, dry, low-energy, lethargic delivery wasn't a device for his act. Steven talked like that all the time.

The man said he was committed to the idea of living for today, for now, in the moment. His life appeared to be uncomplicated and serene, concerned with neither yesterday nor tomorrow. At this point he was a high-income individual, yet he claimed to have no apartment or home.

I believed him when he said his only possessions were a few shirts and jeans, which he was constantly washing.

Steven spent a lot of time in the comedy condo laundry room while his clothes were being cleaned. Not sure if it was the great cycles, round and round, beginning and end, or if it was the sounds of the washing machines, or if he ever physically jumped into a dryer for a spin, but Wright said the process put him in a meditative state. Apparently Steven also liked to play the laundry room change machine, turning dollars to quarters, quarters to nickels and dimes, and nickels and dimes back to quarters. There were better odds than a casino.

I'll always be happy that I once knew sarcastic, nostalgic, reference-slinging politico Dennis Miller. I wasn't one of his close friends, but he always made me feel like one. I worked at clubs with him many times, and I happened to be working in New York when he did one of his first shots on the *Letterman Show*. I accompanied him to the taping, and after, I was with him when he got the great news that he'd be moving from LA to NYC to do *Saturday Night Live*.

What people want to know about Dennis is what made him do a 180 from what was perceived as a liberal reputation to his more recent conservative political opinions. I can't answer that. What I can say is that he always acted hip and casual—but behind that was a steely sort of personality, like if he ever had decided to be president of a Fortune 500 company, he could do it.

At the peak of his *SNL* fame, Dennis did a show with Dana Carvey at Caesar's Tahoe, while I was in the resort next door performing at Harrah's Tahoe. Between shows I met him in the casino as his audience was exiting the showroom. I was amazed by what happened, or rather didn't happen. I thought Dennis was about to be mobbed by fans wanting photos or autographs. Instead, people stood back and just watched Dennis. They were quiet and respectful. If it had been Carvey, he'd have been mobbed by loving fans, but not Dennis. The people looked at him with admiration, but they didn't come too close.

I was walking with him through the casino and he was telling me a story when a guy came running up and asked for an autograph. Dennis said quietly and gently, "You don't want that," and he kept walking and talking with me. The guy wasn't angry—he just stood smiling and watched us walk away.

A promotional company booked me as part of a summer-long series of comedy nights in Los Angeles pubs and bars in front of a sign advertising Metaxa, an exotic Greek liquor. In an effort to raise human blood alcohol content, Metaxa shooters were available for a dollar and you got to keep the shot glass, which displayed the Metaxa logo.

I had no interference as far as my act was concerned, but part of the deal was to use a bottle of Metaxa in one of my tricks, but not to drag it in, to make it seem natural. I of course, said "no problem," but added, for some stupid reason, that I hated the taste of the stuff. To my surprise the guy who hired me said, "Me too." An empty Metaxa bottle, substituted with cold tea instead of the brown alcohol, worked fine for my Grab & Stab trick.

Stuck in a piece of wood were four hunting knives. "Each of these knives has been fitted with a long, sharp-edged metal blade, and each of these knives is a deadly weapon. I am going to have someone take a close look at these, so you can be certain that the knives are real. Sir, would you stand up for just a second? You look like you might be familiar with knives..."

This got an amusing response when I picked a tough or macho-looking guy, which was always done when possible. Next I showed a fifth knife, which appeared identical to the others, but was a fake, one where the blade retracted into the handle.

"Although this pointed weapon is the same size and weight as the others, it won't stick into the wood, and it doesn't cut, because it has a phony blade that allows you to do stuff like this..."

I pushed the knife up my nose, since it was a plastic fakeroo, the blade retracted into the handle, but it looked like the five-inch blade went up my nose. I yelled "Ooooo..." The audience laughed and screamed and then I said, "That's always a crowd pleaser. Don't worry, I've never been wounded... severely."

Next I had the volunteer drop all the knives, including the fake one, into a clear bag made out of very thick vinyl. "Four knives with long, sharp-edged metal blades, one phony one. See if you can keep your eye on the phony knife." I shook the bag vigorously and you could plainly see the knives were hopelessly mixed.

"The name of this game is Grab and Stab! Yes, I'm a fast talker, but I also have the gift to grab. In a moment, I will thrust my hand into the bag, which is dangerous in itself, and the first knife I grab, I will heave into my chest. Aren't you glad you came tonight? I'll grab a knife at random as fast as I can, and I'll do this with such speed, that if I fail to grab the phony one, there will be nothing I can do to rescue myself... so I'll take my applause now!"

There were laughs and cheers, and then I quickly grabbed a knife and stabbed it into my chest, and it stuck. The audience was stunned for a fraction of an instant looking at the knife clearly impaled in my chest. I screamed, "Aahhh! Give me another chance..."

"Don't worry, I've found that a little drink of Metaxa now and then makes a little magic." See how naturally I mentioned that without dragging it in? I pulled out the long knife and grabbed my bottle of Metaxa. "Watch closely." I drank a big swig off the bottle, and a long stream of Metaxa squirted out of the supposed knife hole in my chest. "Enjoy the refreshing taste of Metaxa! It's a great disinfectant!" How about that? A perfectly natural use of Metaxa in a magic trick; I felt so clever.

After a week on the job, my contact at the promo company had the unpleasant assignment of telling me that I was fired. I had been accused, unjustly of course, of denigrating my sponsor's product. Reports had gone to local Metaxa execs quoting me as saying in my show that "I hated the vile taste of the stuff so much it made me attempt suicide." This absurd information was picked up and then thrown back and forth by active tongues. It was like the game of telephone, where one person whispers a message to another, which is then passed through a line of people, and when it gets to the end a bunch of errors have accumulated in the retellings.

I pointed this out and was trying to salvage the ton of money still due on the eleven remaining weeks of my contract, but my arguments were useless. The promo guys said the Metaxa people didn't like me, or my knife trick. They delicately suggested that they had many other clients besides Metaxa, and that if I didn't play rough they would reward me for my good sportsmanship. So I signed an agreement to settle my contract for seven hundred fifty dollars, much less than I had expected to earn that summer.

When I got home, on my cassette tape answering machine, there was an urgent message to go back to the promo office right away. *Well,* I thought, *they didn't waste any time getting me another gig.* I drove back. They had made a staggering

125

error in the release I signed, agreeing to settle my contract, not for seven hundred fifty dollars, but for $75,000! They showed me how a typist had made the mistake and conceded that no one had noticed the wrong amount.

I was an unknown quantity to the promo company and they must have had a moment of panic, wondering what I would do about it. I kidded them a little, but I signed a new release that took them off the hook. Twice in one day I had been a good guy. I was sure my friendliness would pay off, and that they would phone me. And I was right.

True to their word, I got a call the following summer with an offer for another series of comedy nights. We did a deal identical to the Metaxa one, but for Phillip Morris, and the company was happy with my work. Yes, they were a despised organization, their products had warning labels, they were losing lawsuits to lifelong chain smokers with lung cancer, and TV banned tobacco commercials, but, at the same time, cigarette vending machines were very popular, you could smoke indoors everywhere from libraries to grocery stores, and luminaries from Johnny Carson to rock stars to movie idols made smoking look cool and sexy.

My shows were in front of a poster of the then-famous puffing rugged cowboy known as the Marlboro Man. Bar patrons got free butt samples and the product placement in my show was a variation on The Lemon Trick.

I borrowed a dollar bill and the owner signed his name on it. The bill vanished at my fingertips, then a cigarette was broken in half and the signed bill was found inside. Without dragging it in and making it seem a natural intrinsic part of the trick, I bucked the anti-smoking trend by mentioning that medical science had discovered Marlboro's prolonged life, and that the savings are substantial if you buy them by the carton.

Some shows you do for love, others for money. If you can do both at the same time, that's the best, but usually, unless you're in a better financial condition than I've ever been, you have to make a choice. Most times if it pays nice money, like these Metaxa and Marlboro gigs did at the time, you take it.

At Rumors Comedy Club in Winnipeg I did a variation of the old color-changing handkerchief trick, using women's silk panties. I told a story about a girl I knew who was bad at doing laundry—her white panties would come out of the wash green, next wash they'd be yellow, then magenta...she'd say it was the phosphates, the water was full of lime salts, and so on. After the show a pretty redhead came up to me waving some black panties and asked if I could magically change them to pink? I asked her if she came prepared with the panties in her pocket, and she bent over to show me that she hadn't.

Dai Vernon once showed me a postcard I had written to him from Las Vegas. I didn't remember writing it, but he kept it because he liked it. It said, "From here I go to Minneapolis. I always spend my Februarys in Minneapolis."

I used to play at the Rib Tickler in Minneapolis, where they sold barbecued ribs with the jokes. Yes, the weather was cold. The first time I got off the plane, the sun was shining and I said to the guy who drove me, "What a nice day." And he answered, "It sure is. The sun is shining and it's only sixteen below." What he didn't say, was that the wind chill factor made it feel like twenty below...in dog years that's a hundred and forty below.

So, one night I'm onstage at the Rib Tickler, doing a bit called the Insurance Policy. A selected card vanished and then reappeared in my shoe. There was a problem, though. The selected card was the King of Hearts and the card in my shoe was the Three of Clubs.

127

In a panic, I said, "Someday someone's gonna pick the Three of Clubs, and this will be a really good trick..." Then I said, "No worries, I'm covered by an insurance policy."

I took out a pamphlet that had Magician's Insurance Policy written on it, unfolded it, and read aloud the conditions of payment as well as the fine print, "...covers performing magician against failure from warped cards, faulty fingers, rambunctious spectators..." as I read, I kept unfolding until the policy was poster size; when turned around, it showed a big blow-up of the selected card, the King of Hearts.

Sitting alone in the audience, watching me intently, was a guy who didn't seem to be a comedy club regular. For one thing, he was drinking milk. Comedy clubs don't usually do a big milk business. That's the reason he had caught my eye during the show. So it was interesting to see this man swigging milk while everyone else in the room was happily making a sincere effort to raise their blood alcohol content. He seemed to enjoy what I was doing, but he wasn't falling on the floor with laughter.

To this day, after a show I always make myself available to the audience, and nowadays am delighted to shake hands, take a snapshot, or share a minute or two with anyone who cares to. I'm good at it. Not so much so in my comedy club days when it was a bit of a dreaded chore. I did it, but was not always wild about—and most certainly lacked the skill set to properly handle—the extended annoying chatter.

After the show, Mr. Milk came up to me. He seemed to be a very serious man and I imagined that to him comedy and magic were just forms of frivolity. But he was very pleasant, told me he enjoyed my performance, and he shook my hand firmly like he meant business. As I was bidding farewell to others, he continued to stand next to me, like he wanted to speak further. After everyone left, he did.

"Steve, I'm in town with the Prudential Insurance convention and..."

"I'm not in the market for any insurance."

"No, no. I want to buy your magician's insurance policy trick."

I politely declined, but this guy wouldn't give up, "It's a trick I can show clients, a great icebreaker for me..."

"Sorry, I need it for my act, and I can't get another one right away."

He took out a thick bankroll, "I'll pay anything you want." Suddenly the room felt a little icy. This guy wasn't gonna take "no" for an answer. I felt it along my spine, like the wind chill factor. "Here's the money, now give me the policy." Sound a little like the, "Here's the money, gimme what I want," boy named Kevin Grant who bought the Dagger Chest from Femia's Party shop? That's what I was thinking, too. Great minds think alike.

"Okay, the secret is, your clients need to pick the King of Hearts, because that's the card printed on the policy. It's called forcing a card. Here's an easy way to do that; start with the King of Hearts on top of the deck..."

"Don't give me that phony baloney, I want to do it like you did, take a card..."

"You don't get it, the fact is..."

He insisted, so I took one. Milk Man unfolded the insurance policy and showed me the blow-up of the King of Hearts. "Is that your card? No? What? What do you mean no? In the show you said the policy covered you for any card." I quickly explained it's just a trick. But this guy believed it was some sort of real magic insurance policy. He was crushed that the trick was a trick.

"Do you mean to tell me it always shows the King of Hearts? That's no magic, and it's certainly no insurance."

"You were certainly impressed when I did it in the show, otherwise we wouldn't be talking now."

"That's when I thought the policy provided a real service. What kind of insurance covers you for only one card in the deck?"

Pointless wastes of time, like that Milk Man incident, made me averse to mingling and making charming small talk with other minglers and charming small talkers. Despite that fact, however, I've always continued to be accessible after shows, but I'm still not a big schmoozer or even a boozer. Senator Crandall said he had nothing against the people in his audience individually, but rather it was just when they gathered that he didn't like them. I'm the opposite—I love audiences, but individually, sometimes they can be a pain in the drain.

Audiences are number one, except when they treat you like number two.

Fortunately, my decades-old comedy club meet-and-greet phobia has softened to save my butt. Today at Magicopolis I'm no longer the clever young comedy club guy. I'm his older, smarter descendant who understands that questions, offers, conversation, hugs, kisses, clapping backs, autographs, taking photos, gimme five hand-slaps, fist-bumps, and shaking hands are audience compliments akin to applause. It's a pleasure to meet those who like my show and I always make sure to wash my hands before I eat.

TIMOTHY LEARY'S BRAIN

Creating successful comedy and magic routines, and by successful I mean bits that are amazing, get laughs, applause, and are about something, is a trial-and-error proposition. There is no formula, no rules, and no shortcuts.

You think of something that might be interesting or funny or poignant or amazing or all of the above. You build or collect the props, you work out a method to do the trick and rehearse it, you write down what you want to say or do with the trick, and then you try it on stage. What your friends, or mom, or significant other thinks doesn't matter much. You have to try it on stage in front of an audience of strangers.

If it doesn't get laughs or applause and isn't amazing, you try it again, tinker with it. If it isn't what you want it to be, you throw it out and move on. Timothy Leary's Brain was something I wanted to throw out, but like gum stuck to my shoe, I couldn't get rid of it and move on because someone wanted me to do it on a TV special.

This was a routine I wrote and performed that was about sixties icon Timothy Leary and his "turn on, tune in, drop out" promotion of recreational drugs. Furthermore, it was about great artists lost to drug overdoses, like Lenny Bruce, Elvis, John Belushi, Jim Morrison...

The trick that I used to illustrate this dance of words and objects was my version of a classic known as the Chinese Rice Bowls, the same trick I used to watch the Magic Castle's Charlie Miller do while he whistled. In the original, two cereal-size bowls are shown empty. One is filled with rice; the rice then instantly, magically doubles in quantity so it's overflowing into the second bowl. The surprising climax comes when the rice suddenly vanishes and changes into cool, clean water, which is poured from bowl to bowl.

Being an artsy guy, I made what looked like a human brain, which I could split in two, and the brain halves worked the same as the Chinese Rice Bowls trick. The brain was hidden inside a gnarly-looking skull with a removable top. So I could take the skull top off, reach in, and take out my special Chinese Rice Bowls' trick brain.

When I split the left and right brain apart, you could see emptiness inside the two halves. I said, " You know this is Leary's actual brain, because you can see there's nothing in it . . . " Instead of the rice used in the classic trick, " . . . to symbolize those we've lost to drug overdoses," I used "freshly dug graveyard dirt." The brain was rattled; instantly and magically the graveyard dirt doubled in quantity and overflowed into the second brain half. When the dirt suddenly vanished, instead of changing into cool, clean water, the graveyard dirt magically changed to blood, which I poured back and forth between the two brain halves.

In the eighties I was fortunate to be a regular performer at The Comedy & Magic Club in Hermosa Beach. Aside from my thrice annually one-week engagements, when in town I would do short guest spots two or three times a week to work on new material. I'd done my impaired sliced gray matter routine a half dozen times and was ready to throw it in the garbage and go back to the drawing board, when I was approached by a guy from KMEX, a local Spanish language TV station.

"The Brain would be absolutely perfect for our Day of the Dead TV special."

"What's Day of the Dead?"

"It's a Mexican holiday where we reminisce about dead people and how they died. Do you speak Spanish?"

"I don't speak Spanish."

"Too bad; it pays two hundred seventy five bucks."

"I have a friend who could translate and I can learn the bit phonetically."

"Done and done. See you November 2."

I had everything translated and phonetically written on a poster board, practiced, and got it down okay. But I didn't really speak Spanish and certainly couldn't do it without my cheat sheet.

At the studio my cue card was leaned against a bar stool, below the height of the cameras, so it was out of frame. With much trepidation I delivered my routine, and the rehearsal went fine. In fact, it was more than fine. To my great relief, the crew laughed and applauded, the director assured me that I had a great American accent. It seemed to me that Timothy Leary's Brain got a lot better reaction in bad Spanish than it ever did in perfect English.

And then it came time for the actual Day of the Dead TV special performance. With cameras rolling, I was introduced as *mago comediante* Señor Steve Spill. The audience had been told to cheer with enthusiastic abandon. It was my first appearance on KMEX-TV. I felt such warmth and love. It was a sublime moment.

It was at this point that I noticed a blanket of foggy dry ice smoke creeping across the stage. Dry ice is expensive, so it hadn't been there during the rehearsal, but it was now and it was completely obscuring the Spanish words I didn't know. What few words I could see slightly above the foggy dry ice smoke were quickly becoming nothing more than dripping smears of black marker ink. I couldn't read a thing and my performance had to come out on time to the second. No one could understand what I was saying, and the producer signaled me to "Talk slower." As I was running out of time, the signal was "Talk faster."

I struggled through the routine getting it all wrong and looking like a bonehead. There was deathly silence in the studio audience. A loud silence, a hundred sphincters were puckered. Who knows how many were puckered watching it at home on television? I had asked if I could do it again; they said no. There was no taping or filming ahead of time. While I was performing the audience was at home watching. The KMEX Day of the Dead TV special had been a live broadcast, no takeovers. That was the finish of my appearance on Mexican television and the finish of my Timothy Leary's Brain routine.

TRIALS AND ERRORS

Like Timothy Leary's Brain, below are stories in the continuing saga where I had an idea, worked up a method to do the trick, got the props together, scripted the routine, and rehearsed it. But on stage, in front of real breathing strangers, for one reason or another, it wasn't a keeper. Instead, these were routines that turned out to be useless and insignificant. I've included them here because in one way or another I found them to be poetic.

Smoke on the Water—For this one I had a bunch of bells, they were the simple sound-making devices you held in your hand and shook to make them ring. There were eight bells. Each rang a different musical note in the scale. I handed one bell each to eight people in the audience.

In one hand I held a glass of water, and with my other I conducted the orchestra. With the index finger of my right hand, I quickly pointed one at a time to different bell holders. Following my instructions, when I pointed at them, they would ring their bell. When it worked right, the bell ringers played the song "Smoke on the Water," by the British rock band Deep Purple. At the end of the song's melodic hook, a puff of smoke burst from my glass of water.

I thought it was a clever bit and I had fun, but spent a ton of time working it out. When it went as intended, it was great, but sadly most of the time it didn't, largely due to the ineptitude of the inebriated or otherwise impaired bell ringers.

Nose Hair—"Did you ever pull on a straggling nose hair that you just couldn't seem to get out?" I once developed, and had a working prototype, of a tiny spool of thread gimmick, that could securely be hidden inside a nostril. When I pretended to pull a hair from my nose, I would pull on the end of the thread and it would unwind. It looked like I was pulling out a ten-foot hair!

Not a crowd pleaser.

Book Worm—I explained to the audience that prior to my appearance, I wrote one word on a white card and sealed it in an envelope. I taped the envelope to the mic stand so it was in full view. I asked a volunteer to join me on stage to assist in demonstrating my ability to "see into the future."

I handed the helper a dictionary and asked her to examine it and make sure it was ordinary. She gave it back to me, and I handed her a cardboard container, the type you get take-out Chinese soup in, and had her thoroughly examine what was inside. It was full of live night crawlers, the type of earthworms commonly used as fish bait.

As I riffled through the pages of the dictionary I asked my helper to choose any worm and randomly drop that single live worm into the pages of the book, wherever she desired. As soon as she dropped the invertebrate crawler, I slammed the book shut...squishing the worm. The dictionary was then opened to that page; one word seemed to be underlined by the squished worm. I tore open the envelope and the predicted word was the very same one selected at random by the night crawler!

To me, the thing that made this trick great wasn't the dictionary. It was, of course, the earthworms. Although funny, half the time the volunteers screamed, dumped the worms on the floor, tossed them at me or into the audience, or simply refused to pick one up in their hand. This made it impossible to finish the bit. Plus it wasn't so easy to constantly have a fresh supply of live earthworms whenever and wherever I was performing. So, for those reasons, this one ended up in the scrap heap.

Baby Houdini—The Cabbage Patch Doll had a hard plastic head and a soft cloth body. I took the stuffing out of the body of one and replaced it with an inflatable teddy bear. The doll looked normal when blown up, but I could pull the air plug on the back and it would deflate like a balloon with a hole.

I introduced the blown-up doll as Baby Houdini, bound the hands with real handcuffs, the feet with steel chain and an iron padlock, then tied the cuffs and padlocked chain together with a thick rope. As I did this, I said "...in a moment I am going to ask everyone to join me in counting backwards from ten to one...ten, nine, eight, seven...First, I'd like to add that Baby Houdini is not carrying any concealed lock picks or canned ham keys...if anything goes wrong, we do have a trained paramedic GI Joe doll backstage..."

I held Baby Houdini by the head, "Okay baby! Escape!" As the audience counted backwards, the plug was pulled, the doll deflated like a spent balloon, and the connected rope, handcuffs, lock and chain, slipped off, the entire restraint assembly crashed on the floor in a heap. "Tah dah!" My girlfriend at the time thought it was a scream; it always made her hysterical, no matter how many times she saw it. About half the time audiences agreed with her, while the other half of the time the baby deflated along with my ego. Another one bites the dust.

Tainted Clam Mystery—I tried this bit out a few times while appearing at a Cape Cod comedy club that featured a raw bar full of locals cracking open shellfish that were caught that morning. A sack of fresh clams was introduced and a volunteer smelled the clams. Next I had the helper sample the foul aroma of a tainted clam. The rare tainted clam was mixed into the sack of fresh virgin-smelling clams.

The volunteer violently shook up the bag, further shuffling the tainted clam amongst the fresh ones, yet I, the talented one, was able to reach into the sack and instantly bring forth the tainted one. As a prize for assisting, the tainted clam was offered to my volunteer with a little cocktail sauce.

Removable Thumb—I've always liked the "teach a trick" premise. I started by doing the old grandpa-removing-the-thumb trick, using the normal method—the audience saw the back of my hand but didn't see the thumb because it was bent into the palm, and by bending the thumb and fingers of the other hand just right, it looked like one hand took the thumb off the other, an old trick that everyone knows.

Then I gave a bogus, and what I thought was funny, method of how it was done. I held up a blue piece of cardboard, "It's done with a camera trick; first my hand is photographed in front of a blue screen, then model technicians build a thumb, also filmed in front of a blue screen, moving like this." At that point, I brought out a long wire with a fake thumb attached to the end and moved it in front of the blue cardboard. "A robot camera films everything, and after final optical printing, all the elements are put together and the final product looks like this . . ."

For the finish, I again performed the usual old grandpa removing the thumb bit. I thought the premise and execution was hilarious. Audiences responded with, "Meh" and "huh?"

Siegfried & Roy Reenactment—Sometimes performers appear larger-than-life on stage. That was particularly true of Siegfried & Roy. Not so true when I imitated them while using a tricky TV prop that was a pain in the drain to build, transport, and perform. The idea of the bit was that I would show those who couldn't make it to Vegas how Siegfried magically changed a 650-pound Siberian tiger into Roy, and then made Roy vanish.

Wearing a huge Siegfried blond wig, and a humongous over-sized sparkly golden pouch that attached to the front of my crotch—just like the type Siegfried used to wear—I stood in front of a table with a VCR and TV on it. Playing on the TV was a video of a snarling tiger pacing back and forth. I acted like the TV was actually a cage with a live tiger in it, showing, pointing, and gesturing toward the tiger like a girly game show model displaying a new car. As the beautiful animal paced back and forth, I draped a cloth over the TV.

After some appropriate mysterious hand-waving, I whipped the cloth aside. The tiger had vanished from the TV screen and Roy burst into view. It was a great video of him laughing and jumping from some Disney special they had done. I triumphantly covered the TV a last time, more mysterious hand-waving, and when I whisked the cloth away, the TV had vanished. Funny and a great magic trick ending, right? This routine was more work to pull off than you'll ever know, and it didn't even get as good of an audience reaction as the Nose Hair or Book Worm bits.

Disgust is Contagious—In the eighties there were literally a hundred one-nighters in and around the Los Angeles vicinity. Restaurants, bars, hotels, bowling alleys, anywhere that was empty during the week put on a comedy show. I tried out this one in the lounge at the Whittier Hilton. If you were attending that night you would have seen me holding a large pitcher of milk.

"Perhaps some of you have seen the classic bit where a magician takes a sheet of newspaper, forms it into a cone, pours milk into the cone, and the milk disappears. I've developed a new way to do that trick, which I shall now attempt to show you, without gagging."

I quickly drank the half-gallon pitcher of milk. Yep, this part of the routine was identical to the way I drank pitchers of beer in the old rock club act. Next I placed a metal bucket on the floor in front of me and very realistically threw up the half gallon of milk into the bucket. This wasn't a little urp. I puked a half-gallon of milk like a fire hose, and said, "I'm glad I brought that up." People with weak stomachs headed for the exit, and then I picked up the bucket of barf and threw the contents into the crazed audience, drenching many of them, with what was only a bucketful of confetti!

Before I even threw the confetti, as I threw up the milk, a few people in the audience did the same in response. I hadn't expected any audience participation. The bartender yelled for the janitor and there was pandemonium. My hope was for a standing ovation. Instead, I got the smell of fresh alcohol-laced vomit. I guess what goes around comes around. Up to that point, this trick had never elicited more than a loud belch.

As a reward for reading this far in the book, I'm going to expose the three secrets that made this puke routine work so well. The first part is a prop called the Magic Milk Pitcher, which you can buy from a magic store or online, which will allow you to really drink only a cup of liquid but it will look like a half gallon. The Confetti Bucket, which allows you to pour in liquid and throw confetti out, is also available where finer magic props are sold. Now, the best part, the retching part, is my own invention, so without ruffling the feathers of any retailers, I can completely explain it to you...it's done with a cleverly concealed hot water bottle filled with milk.

For those who want to know where on your person to cleverly conceal a hot water bottle filled with milk, and how to use it to simulate realistic vomiting, please buy my next book, which completely covers those questions. That's a lie, but anytime I can get a laugh I'm not going to let the truth interfere with it. Now, where was I? Oh, yeah, I'm writing a book.

PART FIVE

ODDS AND ENDS

LIONS, AND TIGERS, AND BIRDS! OH, MY!

Although I've always loved creatures of all types, personally, with the exception of an occasional moth, I've never used live animals of any kind in my shows. None—neither rabbit nor bird nor tiger. I think animals make bad employees. They are unpredictable, and can die, attack, or poop on your suit at any moment. On the other hand, as anyone who has ever been to a circus or watched a TV chat show with guests from a zoo will tell you, whether you choose animals that swim, dig, creep, or fly, you can count on them pleasing any crowd.

October 3, 2003 was the date of the famous Siegfried & Roy Las Vegas incident where a 600-pound white tiger sank its teeth into Roy and dragged him offstage by the neck. At the time, the first of the numerous official explanations was that the tiger was frightened by a New Jersey woman's big hair. The tiger might have started off meaning to give him a playful nip; we'll never know, since nobody can ever really know what a tiger is thinking. I have appeared onstage with many acts that do work with animals, and also once had a near-death experience with a tiger.

In 1986 I started as a last-minute replacement in *Spellbound* at Knott's Berry Farm in Buena Park, California, and went on to appear in the touring show through 1988 at Harrah's Casino in Lake Tahoe, Nevada and Wild Coast Sun Casino Resort in South Africa. The *Spellbound* shows featured a group of leopards, black panthers, and Bengal tigers. The nucleus of this zoo was leased complete with trainers and handlers from a Hollywood showbiz agency specializing in large carnivorous felines.

One of the first things I appreciated from working in the *Spellbound* show was the nonsense of the common view that showbiz lions and tigers are beaten or drugged into submission—an idea so utterly wrong that it can only be held by someone who knows nothing whatsoever about the animals involved. A lot of people believed that the big cats on stage weren't really dangerous because they were old or had had their teeth removed, but a 600-pound tiger can still gum you to death.

What I'm about to relate took place in South Africa. Since you're wondering, leopards, panthers, and tigers are not indigenous to the continent, so, as usual, the show's professional savage beasts were flown in from California.

The Wild Coast Sun is surrounded by jungle for miles on the three sides that weren't Indian Ocean, with no city and no airport. Most gamblers and vacationers from around the world flew to a big city, like Durban, or Johannesburg, and were bused or taken by limo to The Wild Coast. Next to the resort was a dirt airstrip with several small planes used by VIP gamblers and casino executives.

I was recruited to promote *Spellbound* on a late night TV talk show in Johannesburg, the Manhattan of South Africa, a nearly two-hour flight from the remote Wild Coast Sun. Along for the ride with the pilot and me was a baby tiger named Lulu, weighing in at about 30 pounds, and Nicole, a pleasant animal handler, weighing in at about 110. There is a difference between an animal trainer and a handler. Trainers teach animals something, such as a new trick. Nicole was a handler, so her job was to manage and control the animals. Nicole sat in the cockpit next to the pilot. Lulu was in a carrier next to me, in the rear of the tiny four-seat flying machine.

The plane bounced and bumped like a rubber dinghy on a rough sea. My stomach rose up into my rib cage every time we'd go higher and higher, then suddenly drop a hundred feet. Regardless of whether they were training or handling, everyone involved treated the cats with care and understanding. So I guess it was no surprise when Lulu growled and banged her head against the sides of the carrier that Nicole became concerned and wanted to comfort the little kitty. She turned around, opened the carrier, grabbed the cat, and cuddled it.

In a fraction of an instant, the baby tiger was on the pilot's head, the plane was in a nosedive, and we all had the same instantaneous thought: We are going to crash and die. The plane violently flipped on its side, wedging the squealing kitten between me and the window. Somehow, Nicole and I wrestled the little beast into the carrier. For the next few minutes the grim reality of all this didn't quite hit me. Then I convinced myself I had believed all along that nothing was going to happen to us. There was not a spoken word until we landed. As we deplaned I kissed the pilot. I don't often fly around in small private planes or jets, but when I do, even today, more than twenty-five years later, I go through every second of the little tiger nightmare again.

The late night TV chat show was just like an American one. After my preplanned talk/jokes with the funny guy host, our show's youngest star, Lulu, and her handler, Nicole, were introduced. The cat licked the host's hand, then, as if on cue, leapt onto the host's head. Nicole brought Lulu under control with a morsel of raw meat, but not before she peed on the couch (Lulu peed, not Nicole, or if Nicole also peed, I was unaware of it).

What part did Lulu play in *Spellbound*? Well, at the end of the show, after the cast took their bows, she ran on stage, and that was it. The producer and director felt it added a "cute button" to the production.

A day after the Johannesburg trip, I was still thinking about Lulu's addiction to head humping, and how lucky we all were to have survived that flight. I was thinking those thoughts while bowing to an appreciative audience, when Lulu, playing the part of a cute button, pranced onto the stage, and took a flying leap into the crowd. That was the 30-pounder's final appearance as a cute button. Fortunately, the only injury was to little Lulu's ego.

For me, witnessing this next *Spellbound* cat tail—uh, make that tale—a few times stands out in my memory because it not only features a sleek black panther, but it also features a beautiful showgirl at the top of her game, while simultaneously, it could be said that she was at the bottom of a sewer.

A gorgeous girl in a slinky, skin-tight black dress danced and seductively writhed around on the stage like a wild animal with feline grace. She got into a clear glass box. A cloth hid the woman for a fraction of an instant, and when it was whisked away, in her place, there was a growling black panther. It was a great illusion, but too often this lovely talented lady paid the price.

The cloth concealed a secret compartment that held the panther. Under the cloth cover the compartment gently slid to the bottom of the box, which allowed the panther to make its appearance. At the same time, the girl squeezed into a secret compartment in the deceptively thin tabletop that the box was resting on.

The girl was completely protected from the panther, but she was not always protected from his urine. On those occasions that the savage beast decided to improvise when the cloth was lowered, as if coming from a high-pressure garden hose a bright yellow liquid would be sprayed against the glass walls. To the audience, the yellow wash perhaps looked like an intended part of the trick. Unfortunately, the pee quickly drained into the secret tabletop compartment that hid the girl. When the cloth was whisked away, the relieved panther made his appearance with a mighty growl.

Unbeknownst to the uninformed, the babe's hair, costume, and body were marinating in a sewer of warm panther urine. After the applause, as always, the cat was walked along the apron of the huge casino stage. What followed that was a long choreographed bow where the panther stood on two feet and was rewarded with a piece of raw meat.

By the time the curtain closed, and the glass box was rolled offstage, the girl had been soaking over two minutes in that smelly cesspool, but it must have seemed like days. Big cat urine has a pungent, long-lasting scent that doesn't wash out easy. Sure, she looked like a hot young Playboy centerfold, but she smelled like panther piss. After these episodes, the pretty young lady unleashed a roar that sounded like it came from a tiger's cage at feeding time.

Then there were my experiences with internationally acclaimed dancing chickens at the Teenage Fair, Hollywood Palladium, in 1971. On a tiny outdoor stage surrounded by carnival attractions, several times a day over a long hot weekend, each show started with a fellow teen who played guitar and sang songs. I was the middle act, and the closer, the headliner, was Doolittle Wilder Jr. and his Dancing Chickens.

I did not know then, nor do I now, if the idea for the chicken act and the method of training the chickens went back two generations in the Wilder family, but words to that effect were part of Doolittle's presentation. After a bogus rap explaining the painstaking process of educating and choreographing the fowl, he whisked away a curtain, revealing a large cage sitting on a pedestal. Eight or ten hens were wandering around, cackling and pecking at corn kernels.

Doolittle waved a conductor's baton as the music started. Wings fluttered, kernels began to fly in all directions, and the chickens danced and danced and danced. At his command the music stopped, and there was silence. The poultry had ceased dancing at the last note of music and came to a standstill as if by agreement. Then they went back to wandering, cackling, and pecking, as Wilder stood with his face uplifted, and the assembled onlookers cheered Doolittle Wilder Jr. and his Dancing Chickens. The crowd was unaware that the floor of the cage was actually an electric hot plate, which was powered on and off at the same time as the music. For an encore, Wilder presented his performing rooster. The educated cock—the rooster, although that description also accurately describes the clucker, Wilder, minus the educated part—had a mathematical mind and could count up to six by pecking with its beak on a little bell.

In 1990 I learned the pains of befriending your animal colleagues. I was in a magical revue, Kazzamm, or as I called it, Kablamm, at the Normandie Casino in Gardena, California. In that show, a handsome fellow named Brett Daniels magically materialized humongous macaws, parrots, and cockatoos. Their big, colorful fluttering wings were much more dramatic than the white doves other magicians worked with. When the birds appeared, they flew over and around the audience gracefully before returning to the stage.

One of his birds, a blue and golden macaw named Floyd, was a big fan of mine. I was in the middle of my multiplying fingers routine, where extra fingers kept disappearing from one hand and reappearing on the other, unaware that Floyd was watching me from the flies above. Flies are what we show folk call the ceiling high above the stage that houses hundreds of thick black wires connected to powerful lamps that hang from metal bars, and Brett was offstage trying to get the bird down.

I knew all the beats of my fingers routine, and at a certain point it was obvious to me something was wrong. I hadn't said anything funny, but the audience was laughing, whispering, and pointing. Then Floyd made a perfect landing on my shoulder.

From his vantage point, the macaw alternately checked the fingers I was fooling with and peered at my face, back and forth and back and forth. Floyd was probably picking up a few pointers, and then, with his beak, he plucked a fake finger from my hand, flapped his wings and flew back up to the flies. I was glad he plucked a fake finger instead of one of my real ones. The incident helped make that one of my best performances ever, but the winged benefactor Floyd resigned from my act and went back to working with Brett.

Finally, to wrap up this chapter I'm going to share something that doesn't involve savage jungle beasts or exotic feathered ones, but it does involve a flying creature. This took place in 1991 at the Beverly Wilshire, a hotel, as you might guess from its name, on Wilshire Boulevard in Beverly Hills.

To be more specific, it took place in their hotel ballroom, in front of five hundred people, on a nice, but makeshift, proscenium stage. I mention "makeshift" because this was a portable theater of sorts, and I was told the uneven stage floor led to the accident that created the situation I'm about to share. The occasion was a big birthday bash for March Fong Eu, who at the time was the Secretary of State in California, and I was the magical emcee for this after-dinner show.

Being the emcee, and the only speaking act in this case, made me responsible for keeping things moving once the program started. If something went wrong or for some reason more time needed to be added to the show, the emcee went out and entertained to fill in the cracks.

A beautiful Chinese girl was riding a tall unicycle as if it were a choreographed dance. That would be enough, but then she began tossing metal bowls with her knees and was catching them one at a time on her head. She slipped, fell off her unicycle, and broke her leg right on stage in front of the audience.

The curtains closed and I went out with a rope trick to fill some time while the girl got first aid and the next act prepared to perform sooner than expected. I had plenty of funny to do with the rope trick so I could cover whatever time was necessary. Although the audience just witnessed an accident where a girl was obviously hurt, the job at hand was to go out and get some laughs.

I started fooling with my rope, but the audience was still thinking about the accident. Enunciating in fine style, my mouth was wide open when a fly flew in. It was a big room, not everyone was watching closely, and a lot of folks saw nothing. Closer viewers may have seen a speck, and certainly only the people up front really saw the fly.

The whole audience, though, saw me choked up and coughing, but of course I kept delivering my lines. I received compliments about what a caring person I was. "Mr. Spill was so moved by the plight of that unicycle girl that he was in tears. God bless him," one woman said.

WHEN TRICKS GO WRONG

In 1990 the closing bit to my show, *Magic Trap*, a self-pro-
duced non-extravaganza in a tiny 99-seat Hollywood dump
of a theater, was a parody of the classic Bullet Catch trick. I
did the show six weeks, four times a week, for a total of twenty-four performances. Twenty-three times the routine went
as planned. In the traditional version of the trick, a bullet is
fired directly at the magician, and he catches the bullet—in
a handkerchief, in a bottle, on a plate, or even at the tip of a
sword. I preferred the more contemporary method, catching
the bullet with my teeth.

On stage was a large TV that was an interactive element
throughout the show and provided the finish for my Bullet
Catch routine. Normally, I introduced a former army MP as
my marksman for the stunt. He had a bullet marked by an
audience member so it could be identified later. We stood
facing each other and the marksman fired at my face. The
explosive bang of the shot popped everyone's ears in the
tiny theater. Blood squirted out of my mouth as I collapsed,
apparently dead. There was a horrifying offstage scream, the
curtains quickly closed, the TV lit up, and the audience saw
me deliver this prerecorded onscreen message:

"Earlier today I went ahead and made this video so I
would be able to thank all of you for attending my show. I
never even tried that bullet catch trick before tonight. I just
think it's better to fail at something you love, than to succeed
at something you hate. That's it. Take it easy, everybody.
Thank you. Good night."

So you see, this was a trick planned to go wrong, but one
time it went wrong in an unplanned way. When the marksman pulled the trigger on this particular occasion, nothing

happened. Being the absent-minded bonehead that I am, I had neglected ahead of time to double-check that the firearm had been loaded with the usual blanks. Frantically, he pulled the trigger a few more times, but still nothing happened.

Sensing what was wrong, I did what I usually do when I slip on one of my own banana peelings: I thought of something stupid, in this case, making my cheeks really big and hollering BANG! Instead of doing that, though, I bit the blood capsule that was hidden in my mouth, grabbed my neck, fell to the floor, and screamed something stupid, "There's been a mistake, I'm dying—it was an invisible magic bullet." Someone in the audience shouted, "Invisible magic bullet, my ass; he scared you to death!"

If you were living in Canada in 1986, there is a possibility you may have seen Holiday Magic Spectacular, the only twenty-seven cities, three-month, Canadian tour of a magical revue in which I ever appeared. As was usual when I appeared in these sorts of shows, I was not the star, but merely the token comedy act.

The star illusionist had a very dramatic Houdini-type escape to close the show. The exciting emotional impact of the bit depended in large part on an explosion. That explosion was ignited by a squib, which is an electrical match, in this case, remote controlled from offstage. About a half dozen times during the tour something went wrong and there wasn't any explosion. Bad squib, low remote batteries, bad gunpowder mix, remote interference from an airplane in the area, forgot to press the button—the possibilities were endless.

Dressed as Indiana Jones, our headliner closed each performance with the Coffin of Doom. His feet, hands, waist, and neck were chained to a piece of plywood cut in the shape of a coffin. Attached to the plywood was a bundle of dynamite with a long burning fuse. The coffin, with our star chained to it, was hoisted high above the stage; below was a stuntman's crash pad.

The Indiana Jones movie theme was cranked up to a blasting rock-concert volume. Our guy frantically wiggled around in the chains, showgirls were on the side leaping about, "Hurry, hurry! She's gonna blow!" they screamed. He squirmed, twisted, scraped, jiggered, as he jangled the chains. The fuse quickly burned toward the dynamite. He wasn't going to make it. The girls shrilled, "Oh no! Faster! It's getting close!"

He was just a breath away from being a fountain of gore, when abruptly the music ceased. Eyes bulging, sweat gushing from his pores, wordlessly, expertly, he freed himself from the chains and jumped to safety with only a fraction of an instant to spare. Nothing seems so emphatic as a deafening quiet as when you are expecting the crescendo of a boom, impact, explosion, flames, and the flying wooden shards of a coffin caused by a massive dynamite blast. But in that particular moment of stillness, that dreadful silence, we clearly heard the soft sound of a match that wanted to light, but didn't. Pffftt . . .

Near the end of the nineties, I was the emcee for a big illusion spectacular presented at a convention of Nissan car dealers where the finish didn't go as planned. In rehearsal, our star illusionist made mystical gestures in front of a white picket fence as Nissan theme music played. There was a puff of smoke, and a new Nissan Maxima appeared in front of the fence as a recorded announcement said, "The new Nissan Maxima, built better to last longer." When the Nissan appeared a glamorous showgirl got out and caressed the car as the music came to a crescendo. It was a spectacular illusion and a highly entertaining way to advertise a new car. I knew the audience would be impressed.

Here's how it worked: Before its magical appearance, the car was behind the fence. The background was black and the car was draped with a big black velvet-covered nylon cloth. The Nissan was a super lightweight replica—just a shell of a car on a big skateboard, the heaviest part being the showgirl inside. With the aid of special lighting and under the cover of the puff of smoke, when the announcer said, "The new Nissan Maxima, built better to last longer" the white picket fence opened as a gaggle of hooded stagehands dressed in black whisked away the black cloth covering the car and pushed it into view and the picket fence closed behind it. The illusion required split-second timing to coordinate the lighting, smoke, stagehands, and showgirl.

A thousand dealers from around the world had enjoyed the show, and it was now time for the big finish. Nissan executives were in the front row eagerly awaiting their commercial. They're all excited about the application of magic to their advertising and public-image needs, congratulating themselves on this promotional triumph. Anticipation was high as we saw a puff of smoke and heard the words "The Nissan Maxima, built better to last longer."

Unfortunately, the timing was off. As the smoke cleared one of the stagehands tripped and his end of the black velvet got caught in the door at the same instant the flimsy car was pushed forward. The mix of the cloth pulling one way as the car was being pushed the other way in combination with the girl's actions caused the lightweight door to fall off and the showgirl to stumble forward as the last part of the black cloth was whisked away, taking the front bumper with it. "The Nissan Maxima, built better to last longer."

OUT OF AFRICA

I never had my thirty-second birthday. When you cross the international dateline you lose a day. My birthday is January third. I left for South Africa on the second, 1987, and I landed on the fourth. I never turned thirty-two. I had been there for six months, appearing in *Spellbound*, the afore-mentioned magic and illusion revue show, where I was the token comedy magician.

The venue was The Wild Coast Sun, which was not unlike an American casino located on an Indian Reservation. Sun International's newest resort was located in the Transkei, a vast Tribal Homeland now known as the South African province of KwaZulu-Natal. Tropical heat, white sand, green mountains, rocks, miles of blue water, palm trees, and dozens of different independent native tribes were hidden in the nooks and crannies of the vast thick jungle.

Performing in exotic locations is not unusual for magi-cians and many consider the opportunity for travel a perk. Others travel all over the world and see nothing more than a hotel room and a stage. The show was dark each Sunday and resumed Tuesday evenings, two and a half days each week to explore the mysterious, creeping, crawling, slither-ing, steaming, surrounding jungle. Discovering this new part of the world helped me discover a new part of myself.

Equipped with a tent, sleeping bags, food, and a South African showgirl as my brave guide, the two of us drove on wet dirt roads and thoroughfares into unknown rugged terrain. Waterfalls and rivers cut through the landscape of big green mountains. A couple hours in, we came to an unkempt horseshoe turn, overlooking a beautiful valley and a sparkling river. We turned onto a downward trail, and at the base of that big green mountain, the car got stuck in what turned out to be a foot of mud. There was no one within sight for as far as the eye could see, and this was before cell phones existed so there was no way to call for help.

Before we could even get out of the car, out of nowhere, at least seventy jungle natives appeared. They were elders to kids, an entire village that instantly turned out to see whoever we were. A few were wrapped in shreds of animal skin, others were attired in t-shirts and jeans, some wore small gourds on their genitals or were in loincloths, one guy with dreadlocks had no shoes or shirt and was wearing a black suit with the sleeves pushed up, several wore only the wind, and one wore a cowboy hat.

Not a single one of them looked happy to see us; they all had the same expressionless faces. Maybe we were trespassing on their territory, who knew? Instantly about twenty tribal members surrounded our car, and I suddenly felt convinced that we were going to be killed. But they were not barbarians. The two of us were in a daze looking out the windows, wondering what would happen next. A few seconds later, with their bare hands the jungle crew lifted our car up and out of the muck. We got out of the vehicle with big smiles on our faces, and thanked them profusely. Although many spoke or understood English, others communicated in a dialect exclusive to their tribe.

I picked up a few stones and changed them into small coins with sleight of hand. It seemed like the natives thought it was real magic, but how they could reconcile that thought with the fact that I had no power over a car stuck in mud, I'll never know. The well-spoken English-speaking witchdoctor wasn't exactly fooled by my coin trick, but was happy for me to give him a quick instruction and said it was a clever secret. As a gift, I offered a scholarly little book I had in the car, *Maskelyne on the Performance of Magic*. He replied, "To what purpose? You can read the moon, the heavens, the deepest jungle, the sun, and the rains. Enough is written there, more than in any book."

The witchdoctor took us down and around a dirt trail to the tribe's hidden valley village. At first it seemed to be a bit of a frightening journey, but also alluring. Their homeland, not on our map, was an oasis in the middle of nowhere. A cluster of perhaps a couple dozen round structures were made of stones and clay with thatched roofs, some made of branches and animal skins, others were woven structures that resembled massive inverted baskets—all surrounded by farm land, cattle, chickens, and goats. We saw women and even kids carrying their body weight in firewood on their heads, working crops with primitive-looking tools.

There was a generator—they had some electricity, but when we went to this village, we still went back in time. At nightfall, with a purple liquid gulped from coconut shells, we washed down chunks of a cow or a goat, not sure which, that had been buried in the hot coals of a fire. We shared the ham, cheese, bread, applesauce, peanut butter, and dates we'd brought with us, which were savored as delicacies by the witchdoctor, the chief, and three of his wives.

Next it was jungle boogie time. Pounding drums of every size and shape, a wooden bar xylophone, cymbals, gongs, and everybody danced and danced and danced. We camped on their grounds and stayed the entire next day and night and it was a fascinating experience living with the tribe. I was persuaded to join in a spear-throwing game. They had a gourd, which they rolled on the ground, and threw spears at it as it went. I tried it and failed miserably, but eventually got the hang of it and put the spear right through the middle of the gourd.

We established an easy relationship with the tribe and that night we sat around the fire telling stories; some were interpreted into English for us, and some of what we said was translated into their language for others. We learned they'd had the option to settle in a village associated with modern society, but elected to live in relative isolation. So it was surprising, when I announced we'd be leaving early the next morning, to learn that, in spite of that decision and their appearance, they had a considerable amount of money.

One elderly tribesman, who wore overalls and sunglasses, offered the equivalent of fifty dollars in cash to take him with us. Of course we gave him a lift for nothing. At dawn the next day, we were back on the road, with the old man, but not before I promised the tribe we'd be back to do a little magic show for our saviors. I knew my witchdoctor-themed Voodoo Doll trick was tailor-made for this audience. When I had developed it for use in comedy clubs, it never occurred to me I might actually perform it in the presence of a real African witchdoctor.

After about an hour on the road, our senior tribesman told us the witchdoctor had inherited his title from his father, the former tribe witchdoctor, who had passed on. He went on to tell us that the newer, younger witchdoctor "was a man of much wind and little magic." In those distant days, apparently the father's charms were prized. Offerings were left for him daily, and feasts were given to celebrate his most successful oracles. He was counselor, magician, mediator, and teacher to a generation.

We, of course, were immediately intrigued. "You must teach the son some great magic. Understand? Tricks. So he can demonstrate to the young ones his mighty power, and regain the prestige his father had." The old guy clung to old memories and traditions. He seemed to believe the younger generation was going to the dogs. Recalling what the witchdoctor said about reading "the moon and the heavens" when I shared the secret to the stones to coins trick and offered the gift of my magic book, I didn't think that I'd have any success honoring the elderly native's request. But I promised to give it a try. Then our senior tribesman asked to get out, and we dropped him off in the middle of nowhere. Later we heard that was his first ride in a car and that it made him a little sick, but he liked it. The showgirl and I were both back onstage in *Spellbound* at the Wild Coast

Casino, but the following week we returned to the village to present a little magic show.

The natives gathered, the men apart from the women. Mothers with infants and kids were at the back, and in front was the witchdoctor, who declared, "One witchdoctor in a tribe is enough, I think, but it is true that this man is here in fun and does not possess true powers, so let the entertainment begin." My bits with ropes and paper and handkerchiefs went well, as did my needle swallowing. I closed the performance with my Voodoo Doll, and I made our witchdoctor the star of the routine.

I drew a simple face—essentially a big oval with two eyes, a nose, and a mouth—on a big artist's sketchpad, and leaned the pad against a tree stump so the crowd could see the face. I then showed a stuffed burlap doll.

"Watch what happens when we expose one of the doll's eyes to a flame." The witchdoctor held the flame from a lighter under the doll's eye, and one of the eyes on the sketchpad burst into flames. I joked, "Okay, who brought the marshmallows?"

A word about my jokes—no one laughed, not everyone understood what I was talking about even when I wasn't joking, but out of habit I stuck to my usual script which kept the rhythm to my performance intact, and kept me from losing track of what I was doing.

I blew out the burning paper. "Now the hat pin..." Next the witch doctor poked the doll's other eye with the pin, and the corresponding eye on the pad of paper dripped blood. "Well class, we've lost another pupil."

"Got your nose!" I pretended to take off the doll's nose, and the drawn nose on the pad visibly slid off the paper. When I tore the paper drawing off the pad to give to a kind audience member as a gift, the head of the doll fell off its body and onto the ground. And that was it.

The witchdoctor picked up the doll head and looked carefully at the spots that he had poked and burned, then bowed to me, and decreed the demonstration to be good and interesting, but added, "This doll couldn't possibly cause harm or death to an enemy without the advice or charms of a true witchdoctor."

Then he drew a circle in the dirt with his staff, and borrowed a bracelet from a young woman. She obliged after a guarantee that the trinket would be safely returned. He set down a melon beside the bracelet and covered the objects with a blanket. Some pungent herbs were burned, he beat the ceremonial tom-tom, and then the young witchdoctor went into a brief trance, chanted, and confirmed he was in contact with the sacred ancestors. Then he lifted the blanket. The bracelet had disappeared. The melon was sliced open and in the center was found intact the girl's bracelet. Yep, another variation of the old Lemon Trick, and I was pretty sure this version wouldn't be appearing on any instructional videos. The assemblage acclaimed him and my guess is, some prestige was restored.

The tribe was so enthralled, so bewildered, so enthusiastic, that I can't imagine there ever being a better audience for a magic show ever. It was a most gratifying honest to goodness kumbaya experience. Ever since, I've always measured the quality of shows I've done not only on whether they were successful in terms of artistry or cash or publicity, but also by what the actual experience of doing them was like. Seldom has the memory of any other performance stayed afloat this long, and this vividly, in my recollections.

There is a movie, *The Gods Must Be Crazy*, in which a Coke bottle falls from an airplane and profoundly changes the lives of a native tribe. In this case, the tribe was the Coke bottle that changed me forever. I still cherish that feeling of warmth and the sound of their surging roar of enthusiasm for my performance, a sound that no other audience has. As I type these words, I am touched again by the memory.... I've learned to re-create that sound in my head and replay it whenever I need a personal standing ovation.

There were plenty of other performances for me at The Wild Coast Sun Resort & Casino, but none as rewarding as that night with the natives. Several months down the line a panicked call came from my parents. They asked if I was okay, since they read in the *LA Times* that a coup had occurred in the Transkei. "Really? I hadn't heard about that." When I asked, the casino entertainment director said, "Nobody pays much attention. Now and then, a different tribe, with a new chief, takes over the Tribal Council. They don't hold elections, they have coups."

PART SIX

AND NOW A WORD FROM OUR SPONSOR

YES I CANNES

Larry Wilson is a successful and funny stage performer and in 1986 he landed an assignment that required him to do close-up sleight of hand with cards. Magicians perform under a variety of circumstances. At the time, this area was new to Larry. So I came to the rescue and gave Larry a crash course on how to do close-up sleight of hand with cards.

Mr. Wilson had been hired to appear for twelve days on the French Riviera at the world's most famous film festival, the Cannes Film Festival. He had been engaged to do tricks with playing cards that had been specially printed for Empire Entertainment, which at the time was a producer of low-budget exploitation films. The Empire decks had fifty-two different films depicted with movie posters, a different one on each card. Essentially, each playing card was a business card for a different movie title. The only two films in the entire deck that actually existed at that point in time were the King of Hearts and the Ace of Spades, as the movies *From Beyond* and *Re-Animator*.

The other fifty films depicted, with titles like *The Last Los Angeles Virgin* and *Cosmic Chopper Chick Ninjas*, didn't actually exist. The idea was to use those titles and poster art to pre-sell the theater, video, broadcast, and cable rights worldwide. The Empire mantra was, "If you can't pre-sell it for enough money, don't make the movie." The goal with presold films is often to make a profit before they're even released.

The Cannes Film Festival on TV shows like *Entertainment Tonight* is about big stars and award-winning films. On the French Riviera it's also about buying and selling movies. For every Universal Studios and Warner Bros there are dozens of companies like Empire. The majors get attention with movie stars, big-time directors, and awards. The little guys use other methods like direct marketing and publicity stunts, but I'm getting a little ahead of myself here.

As I mentioned, the year was 1986, and the festival started in May. In April, Steven Spielberg and Martin Scorsese cancelled their plans to attend, due to fears of Libyan terrorism and the unknown results of the nuclear accident in Chernobyl that had just happened. Some big American movie stars also cancelled, as did Larry Wilson.

Some stars and directors backed out, but the movie companies did not. Charles Band, president of Empire Entertainment, summed it up for many, when he said, "We're not risking radiation and terrorism for nothing. We're going over there to do business."

Larry was out, and I was in. This wasn't sloppy seconds by any means. I was thrilled to have the opportunity, and it turned out to be one of the best gigs ever. Empire wasn't the biggest company, but I was limo'd from the airport, given cash in hand per diem for pocket money, my hotel included complete carte blanche for room service, and I was treated like a star.

Every day I was whisked to several locations where I performed card tricks on a black velvet tabletop, and pretty girls handed out free decks of Empire cards. The locations were in and around the main festival hotels—the Martinez, Carlton, Concorde, Hotel du Cap, The Croisette, the Palais (where the awards were given), the American/British/Canadian pavilions, and numerous parties, hospitality suites, and bars.

Entrance to the pavilions and participating hotels was permitted by festival badges, and at more exclusive gatherings names were checked against a guest list and given walkie-talkie clearance—those were the events where movie fans, held back by ropes, lined either side of the entrances and stared at me accusingly, their cameras poised for that photo opportunity: Who are you? Are you famous, and if not, why not?

The independent companies worked this same circuit with all kinds of schemes designed to get badge-wearing acquisition attendees to become aware of their firm's films. T-shirts were common give-aways, and some companies relied on eight-foot bears in full costumes, a Rambo look-a-like with machine gun, topless girls, stunts, and crazy happenings to entice attendees.

I'm not sure if it's because that year there were fewer stars, or if it was always like this, but the whole bunch of us were constantly photographed, televised, and people could never do enough for you. It was the most extraordinary display of ego-stroking that I'd ever seen. A photo of me with a playing card on my face appeared in *Paris Match*, and in the *Daily Variety* distributed to conventioneers, I ended up in the column *Buzz du jour*.

And let's face it, the companies we represented were selling films with a lot of action and nudity and very little dialogue. They were definitely not award-winners. They were, however, the type of movies that attracted viewers of all languages with a minimum of dubbing. I heard critic Roger Ebert swear he even met a man selling films like ours by the pound.

Actor Bob Hoskins put his autograph on a card, *Boston Bimbo Invasion*, and shuffled it back into the deck. I tossed the deck to the ceiling high above everyone's heads at the Hotel du Cap...and abracadabra! The signed card stuck to the ceiling while the rest of the deck came fluttering down. A day or two later I was doing my thing at another gathering, when Hoskins came up with a few buddies and said, "Do that card on the ceiling trick you did for me for my friends." The joke was that at that moment I was outdoors performing on the deck of a pirate ship.

The purpose of my out-and-about performances was to raise awareness of the Empire brand and encourage likely clients to consider visiting the Empire hospitality suite. Every company had a suite; they were ordinary hotel rooms with wide open doors. Ours was in the Martinez, the normal beds removed, and in their place were a few couches, wide screen televisions, and the walls were adorned with posters depicting movies that were for sale. The suites entertained a constant flow of potential buyers who could socialize while quaffing complimentary cocktails, see the posters for future releases, preview sample reels of upcoming movies, and get passes to screenings of completed films. Of course, salesmen were available to close deals.

A fixture in our suite was Brian Yuzna, the producer of Empire's big success from the past year, *Re-Animator*, a science fiction horror comedy based on an H. P. Lovecraft story. Yuzna was also the producer of that year's hot ticket, *From Beyond*, also a science fiction horror comedy based on an H. P. Lovecraft story, and was presently pre-selling to raise funds for *Dolls*, his next science fiction horror comedy. When not elsewhere, I was often in the suite doing card tricks, likely ones that pointed out Yuzna's great work and led to me introducing him; then he would pick up the ball and pitch his wares.

Here's how it worked: A selected card vanished and then reappeared in my shoe. But there was a problem—or so it appeared. The selected card was the King of Hearts with a poster depicting *From Beyond* and the card in my shoe was the Ace of Spades with the aforementioned *Re-Animator*. "...and, here is your card... *Re-Animator*, a great choice... what? You didn't pick *Re-Animator*? Too bad, last year *Re-Animator* was a worldwide winner that returned exhibitors as much as a four to one profit on invested dollars."

In a panic, "No worries, I'm covered by an insurance policy." I took out a pamphlet, identical to the one I wrote about in the comedy club chapter, that had "Magician's Insurance Policy" written on it, unfolded it, and read aloud the conditions of payment as well as the fine print, "...covers performing magician against failure from warped cards, faulty fingers, rambunctious spectators..." as I read, I kept unfolding until the policy was poster size. When turned around, it showed a big blow-up of the selected King of Hearts advertising Yuzna's newest, *From Beyond*.

"Obviously you know what you're doing, sir. You've picked a winner, *From Beyond*... I'm insured for card tricks, and our clients are insuring their success with *From Beyond*, which is projected to easily equal or surpass *Re-Animator* profits, and right this very second is the perfect time to get in on the ground floor of *Dolls*, which is destined to be Yuzna's next big hit. And now it's my pleasure to introduce you to the man behind these money-making films. Please say hello to Mr. Brian Yuzna." And that was how I so naturally mentioned Brian's name, in the context of the magic trick, of course.

MORE ASIANS

In 1990, shortly after wrapping up my engagement as the token comedy magician in a revue show called *Kazzamm*, at the Normandie Casino in Gardena, California, I was out of work with nothing on the immediate horizon. I knew I could bounce back, but I had to figure out how. The solution was to continue my employment with the Normandie, a stable, well-paying organization. The problem was that they weren't offering me another job. Well, I came up with an idea I thought was an absolutely brilliant way to create a little work for myself.

The Normandie is a poker club. There aren't any slots, roulette, or craps...it is pretty much just poker. And this began before poker was a hot TV sport, and before the California invasion of the Indian casinos that have a smorgasbord of games. Besides ponies and the lottery, this was one of only a handful of places in the entire state with legal gambling. And the majority of gamblers seemed to be engaged in a crazy poker game called Pai Gow. It wasn't long before I'd noticed that, day in and day out, more than half the gamblers in the casino are Asian, and they're all playing Pai Gow.

Over the years I've pitched all kinds of ideas; this was the first one that had any sort of racial component. The Normandie entertainment director and the company's publicist were on-board with my new idea and through them I got five minutes with the big shots at the weekly meeting.

"You can go in now, Mr. Spill." I was ushered into the conference room. Around the table sat a dozen men. The casino owner, Russ Miller, rose up from the head of the table and shook my hand. He smiled, "Go ahead Steve, I'm listening. What's on your mind?" "Well, actually sir, it's a target-marketing plan. As a goodwill gesture, the casino sponsors me to go out to various Asian organizations each week and perform my one-man comedy magic show. Audience members get a voucher redeemable for chips in the casino and free tickets to the Incredible Acrobats of China in the casino showroom. Through a friend, magician Mark Wilson, I can book the acrobats."

Nobody spoke for a moment. In the stunned silence I remember seeing the light go on in the dozen pairs of eyes around the board table. It was like, could this thing possibly work? There was a long pause. "Congratulations. I like it. Let's do it," said Miller, rising to his feet. I felt exhilarated. It was a sweet deal. The Normandie gets a fresh supply of visitors, and I get a commission on the acrobats and a bunch of one-night engagements that come with decent pay. Miller agreed to an eight-week test—seven weeks on the road for me, and one week in the showroom for the acrobats. A very cool full-color mailer was printed with great artwork, my bio, and details about both my one-man show, which we called *Night Magic*, and the upcoming acrobat show at the Normandie. When the casino public relations person followed up the mailer with phone calls, the response was good. Suddenly I had four gigs a week for the next seven weeks—the Korean Ski Club, Chinese Chamber of Commerce, National Karate Alliance, Thai Herbalist Conclave, and so on. The shows went great, casino executives monitored what I did, and they seemed to like what they saw. Thousands of acrobat tickets and gambling vouchers were distributed.

Yet just nine of the tickets distributed at my shows were used. Three vouchers were redeemed for casino chips. The program had been a complete failure. And thus ended my foray into the world of target marketing.

MR. EXEC

Beginning in the nineties, I periodically performed at corporate events. Typically they are after-dinner shows in hotel ballrooms presented to badge-and-briefcase conference types who work at tech companies, investment organizations, and banks. My client list has also included major retailers and pharmaceutical firms. In total, I've probably done at the very least a hundred-plus of these forgettable gigs. Food is consumed, coffee is poured, and the show begins. As a rule, nothing out of the ordinary has ever happened, except for some rare exceptions.

One such exception occurred years back, when a company thought it would be a fun idea if the corporate executives performed as entertainers at one of their company parties. I was hired to train one of them to do a magic act. Mr. Exec wanted me to teach him to make a girl vanish on stage, then have that very same girl instantly appear in the audience, just like he'd seen me do in our show at Magicopolis. I told him the vanishing act was doable, but after checking it out, the instantaneous appearance of that very same girl in the middle of the ballroom at this particular hotel wasn't feasible—unless maybe we could do the trick with identical twins? Mr. Exec thought that was a fine idea, and a fine pair were cast and rehearsed at Magicopolis.

The next morning I was scheduled to meet Mr. Exec for breakfast before our final rehearsal with the twins in the hotel ballroom. Upon my arrival I was informed that Mr. Exec had left a message for me to come up to his hotel room.

I knocked on the door, and there was no answer, but the door was unlocked, so I walked in to an empty living room. Some sound was coming from the bedroom, so tapping on the door I said softly, "If you're not up yet, I'll see you later in the ballroom." He answered, "No, Steve, come on in."

As I entered, there was Mr. Exec in bed with one of the twins. Not in the mood to watch, I turned to leave, and the guy gasped between moans of pleasure, "Don't go, Steve, we'll only be a few minutes." I quickly left and closed the door, but not before I discovered where the other twin was—under the sheet at the foot of the bed, adding to Mr. Exec's ecstasy.

Don't believe anyone who tells you that the lives of captains of industry are all work and no play.

PART SEVEN

MAGICOPOLIS

GROUNDBREAKING TO GRAND OPENING

Whatever small place I have in posterity is due mainly to the creation and operation of Magicopolis and its improbable and amazing seventeen-years-and-counting history. The first time the project popped onto anyone's radar was back on Wednesday, March 25, 1998. I was at 1418 Fourth Street in Santa Monica, along with members of the media, including CNN, local affiliate NBC, CBS, ABC, FOX news field reporters, and morning show camera crews, including *The LA Times, LA Weekly*, and *Daily Variety*—the occasion was the groundbreaking ceremony for a new theater devoted to the craft of magic. "MAGICOPOLIS," the new sign read, with yellow lettering, shadowed in red, against a black field. My brainchild—Magicopolis.

For years I've been asked where the name came from. My stock answer is that "Magicopolis" is the Greek word for "home of the finest magic show on earth." The truth, though, is as follows: I needed a name that hadn't yet been a registered trademark, and fast. Houdini's?—taken. Magic Castle?—no go. Wizardz?—sorry. That's when I got the idea to make up a word. But not just any word would do. It would have to be a word that would mean city of magic. Magicopolis—it was a mouthful to say and not that catchy, but it worked for me.

I had talked to a great many people about my Magicopolis idea, mostly the wrong people. But enough people kept talking about it and the right people began to think it was a good idea. A ton of time was spent coaxing and cajoling, enticing and exhorting, leading and luring, inducing, prodding, tempting, and tantalizing millions of mankind to do millions of things. This was before the era of Internet crowd funding, so, interested or not, each of those millions had to be spoken to personally, individually, and convincingly, to get the millions necessary for the project.

The Mayor and City Council were persuaded to proudly proclaim the date of our groundbreaking Magicopolis Day in Santa Monica, I had convinced Penn & Teller to make a special appearance at the event, been granted a permit to demolish the 10,000 square foot interior of this address, and construction plans for my showplace had been approved. Together with the luck of a slow news day, these factors propelled the Magicopolis groundbreaking ceremony into the LA media spotlight.

Me, Penn & Teller, telling lies at press conference announcing the groundbreaking of a theater devoted to the craft of magic.

Reigning Santa Monica mayor Robert T. Holbrook took the podium, welcomed the crowd, and read the proclamation declaring March 25, 1998 to be known as Magicopolis Day in Santa Monica.

Flashback to January 1995. It was a Tuesday afternoon, and I was amid a blur of gigs, on a plane, staring out at the clouds, when a life-changing notion came to mind. I was forty years old and living my dream, but the thing was, even though my work didn't require getting up before the crack of dawn every morning it was starting to feel like a nine-to-five job. Working hard was not the problem, but I wanted more independence, to answer only to myself, to not depend on others for work. It was those things, and a couple of little problems that gave me the most important idea of my life.

One problem—I was technically living in Santa Monica, but only spending a handful of nights per month in my own bed. I felt like Santa Monica would always be my home, but unfortunately I wasn't at home often. Instead of constantly changing cities to find new audiences, I needed a way to stay home more and have new audiences constantly find me.

The other bothersome problem, as sure as my name isn't Harry Houdini, was that most of my audiences were not coming to see me in particular—or even a magician in general. I was a corporate event entertainment, or doing a comedy spot in a variety or revue show. Even when I was a headliner, it was often at a comedy club where one went to see comedians and might be surprised the show was topped by a magician.

These ideas rolled around in my head constantly—while on planes, in cars, hotel rooms, eating, sleeping, and breathing. I thought so hard my brain hurt. The idea to produce, and perform my own show, in a theater I designed, built, run, and named Magicopolis, was not born suddenly. It grew gradually in my mind, but it was a Tuesday in April, 1995 that I knew that was what I wanted to do. I yearned for the intoxicating freedom of being a servant of nobody.

Day after day the voices rose and the drumbeats tap-danced in my skull. I wanted Magicopolis to be professional, to be imaginative, and to do something people would get a kick out of. Then I'd back down, racked with doubt. What did I know about supervising construction and decoration, plumbing and electrical;

organizing suppliers and equipment, staff; arranging publicity and advertising and printing, lights and sound, and all the other thousand-and-one tasks for which I had no previous experience?

There were a million reasons not to do it and I ignored all of them; those million reasons crashed to the floor of my brain with the clatter of tin cans, and there was no turning back. I had the power. I wasn't so interested in power as I was in doing something the way I wanted to do it. I wanted control. My power was the courage and audacity to believe in the Magicopolis idea, and the stamina to follow it through and make it a reality.

The Rolling Stones are famous for their phrase about how you can't always get what you want, but if you try, sometimes you get what you need. Well, I'm here to tell you that sometimes you can get what you want and what you need at the same time, but it has its trade-offs. Driven and unable to relax, I guzzled triple espressos and gave up a few things I really enjoyed doing to devote all my time to working on the project. You know, things like eating, sleeping, and breathing.

Flash forward to March 25, 1998, the press conference portion of the ceremony commenced, with me describing the project and answering questions. Next, I pointed to a faux brick wall and introduced "the two most important men in magic, Penn & Teller." There was a puff of smoke, a cymbal clash, and like cartoon characters, the duo burst through the wall leaving holes, exactly the same shapes as themselves, like silhouettes.

What happened between the conception of the idea and that day in 1998 is something else I couldn't have predicted. I fell in love with the stunning, smart, compassionate, talented, Polish actor/writer Bozena Wrobel. She would become my best friend, my wife, my lover, and my partner in crime in Magicopolis. It was a November night in 1997 when we met, and she was celebrating her birthday at Igby's, a West LA comedy club. My act had gone well, and when I came off stage I saw her at the bar, smiling at me. She looked as though she could give a man something that he needed to quiet his soul and soothe his body.

I was saying inside myself, "I am incomplete. She would make me complete. I wonder..."

Then Bozena opened her mouth and began talking in her own peculiar brand of broken English, and a great belly laugh came out of me. It's hard to make me laugh. I observe, I smile, but when I'm really amused you can hear me a block away. My vanity was tickled with a thousand feathers when she spoke my name. Before her accent became a little more Americanized, instead of Steve, when she said my name it sounded like "Stiff!" Everyone within earshot always thought I was a real stud muffin, which I was perfectly willing to accept.

She stared at me with wide eyes and has been looking at me with wide eyes ever since, except for the many times when she closed her eyes to my errors and my faults. Bozena intently listened to my grandiose Magicopolis scheme. I took her to the empty building on Fourth Street, and with spray paint cans we drew on the floor where the stage would be—we drew the walls, lobby, and dressing rooms. The project was a constant topic of conversation. Besides her physical beauty and inward loveliness, Bozena had intelligence—and brains help in the long-range plan of happiness.

Just a few months after we met, on a romantic weekend, I pulled a rabbit out of a hat. They say one of life's most memorable moments is a man asking a woman to marry him. I don't remember

Karolina Wrobel

Bozena is the love of my life. I admire Polish women because they speak a foreign language so well.

proposing to her; I have no idea how it happened, but I do know it was a spur-of-the-moment, totally impulsive idea that Bozena agreed to. I remember the wedding—it's etched into my credit card bill forever. We flew to Vegas and were married at a drive-thru wedding chapel, with a drive thru-reception at Jack in the Box. There was no throwing of rice, no clergyman, and no bantering by envious wedding guests. The total time on the taxi meter ran us to thirty-nine dollars. Marrying Bozena was the best thing that ever happened to me.

Now back to March 25, 1998. To conclude the groundbreaking festivities, Penn & Teller cast their hand and footprints in wet concrete and autographed their work. That night, and over the next few days, various media outlets aired clips of the brick wall bit and handprints which put the Magicopolis name in front of the public. Their autographs and prints remain in our lobby today, as does the fake brick wall with the cut-outs of their silhouettes. Six months later, Penn & Teller lent their celebrity to generate even more publicity for Magicopolis by presenting their show at our grand opening.

Now if I can only manage to figure out a way to turn Magicopolis Day into an annual holiday, where there's no mail, banks are closed, and everyone has the day off to see a show at Magicopolis, I'd be a happy man.

The business at hand, however, entailed a relentless six months dealing with a general contractor and various subcontractors from soup to nuts—mechanical, structural, electrical, plumbing, framers, cabinet makers, curtain makers, general and theatrical lighting, concrete, glass, and others capable of performing the multifarious tasks necessary to bring all the elements together into the final Magicopolis realization. There were a lot of people involved, and I was acutely aware that all their eyes were on me. I had to learn how to deal with having authority over a ton of workers, which was nerve-racking. Dealing with all these different personalities and egos was an eye-opening experience.

Essentially I had to be not only a magician but a juggler as well.

The buck stopped with me and I learned the advantage of saying "No." A negative can be salvaged more easily than an affirmative in so many of life's affairs. I became extremely careful to look before leaping, and seldom said, "Yes," or, "No," but found myself often saying things like "Maybe," or "I'm not sure," or "I'll let you know later." No matter what decisions I made, it was likely someone would be upset.

Hearing "No" or "Maybe" or "I'll let you know later" in response was hard for me to swallow. But I wasn't going to be defeated by a negative or indecisive answer. If I couldn't convince someone of something, I just accepted it and moved forward. True, I had occasional bursts of temper, but on the whole I was methodically persistent and whenever there was a needed compromise it was done my way.

That very afternoon, immediately following the groundbreaking ceremony, marked the start of our demolition. When people hear the term "demolition," the first thing that likely comes to mind is an explosion, or the sight of an entire building crumbling to the ground. In the case of 1418 Fourth Street, it was an interior demolition that was required, leaving the exterior of the structure intact, an immense undertaking that took a week.

Transforming a former record/video rental warehouse into a theater complex required new everything, which meant removing drywall, stud walls, concrete, digging floor trenches, removing slabs, and dismantling virtually every interior part of the structure including all plumbing and electrical. The only thing that remained after the week ended was the square of concrete with Penn & Teller's paw prints.

I wrote "new everything," but a lot of the items newly installed were salvaged from other buildings that were being torn down or renovated, a fun and valuable tip I picked up in my youth from the Castle's Milt Larsen. The Santa Monica building & Safety approval and plan check process took a year, which gave me ample time to collect things like

ninety-year-old theater seats (originally in an Orpheum theater, then a monastery), some magical stained glass, various
bits of antique hardware, old wood, a couple of Dutch street
lamps, and other eclectic building supplies.

Building & Safety approval was among the first of many
dozens of approvals, compliances, demands, and official
requirements by various city, county, state, federal, and private entities. Weekly a plethora of inspectors monitored,
measured, calculated, and tested each and every elemental
increment of the new strucutre.

As the opening date grew near, I was hounded daily by
dozens of salesmen of every sort, ASCAP demanded licens-
ing and advance royalty payments for our future use of any
music, and I was besieged by twenty-five magicians a week
soliciting work with audition videocassettes and follow-up
phone calls. A magic show technically does not come under
their terms, but somehow as a performer I was in violation of
Actor's Equity Association rules for not signing a union contract with the theater's owner or show's producer. In other
words, the union wanted me to sign a contract with myself. I
told them I'd decided to fire myself for not signing.

Flash forward to opening night, Friday, September 18,
1998. The evening itself, clear and warm, as Santa Monica
often is in September, was one big sparkle with the return of
CNN, local affiliate NBC, CBS, ABC, FOX news and morning show camera crews, the *LA Times*, *LA Weekly*, *Daily
Variety*, and several national outlets all were on the red carpet at Fourth Street for the grand opening of Magicopolis.

Long before the opening hour, an imposing throng gathered in front of the theater. No tickets were sold; the tickets
for the opening had been distributed to a select list well in
advance, and most of those outside who vainly tried to get
in had no chance whatsoever of doing so, but they kept on
trying. For the most part the crowd had to content itself by
glimpsing a splattering of celebrities, kind of like law enforcement did when they kept track of mourners at mob funerals
in the *Godfather* films. Cameras captured LA's glitterati and

opening night attendees from popular TV shows of the day like Jeri Ryan from *Star Trek: Voyager*, Wallace Langham from *The Larry Sanders Show*, Paul Provenza from *Northern Exposure*, and Hercules himself, Kevin Sorbo.

I welcomed the crowd and kicked off the festivities. Then, in an effort to squeeze the absolute maximum promotional value out of this momentous occasion, that opening night audience witnessed the brilliance and power of the legendary Penn & Teller. To further broaden the media reach, it was Julie Moran from TV's *Entertainment Tonight* who hosted the show and allowed herself to be levitated by those bad boys of magic. Penn & Teller performed all my personal favorites from their voluminous repertoire of mind-bending greatest hits.

Strangling an innocent boy who left unharmed due to his belief in Teller's ability to perform religious miracles, Penn playing bass while Teller exposed the complex modus operandi behind what looked like a simple cigarette trick, Teller accidentally impaling Penn's hand with a buck knife to reveal a selected card, and a plethora of other daring, provocative, refreshing entertainments.

Penn & Teller had the audience in the palms of their hands and weren't about to turn them loose. Over the cackling, chanting, cheering, clapping, shuffling, and stomping, Penn simultaneously ate fire and used his commanding voice to deliver a heartfelt discourse on the value of seeing magic performed live and the importance of Magicopolis. At the finish of the show I came out and made a speech of thanks to the distinguished audience. As soon as we were alone, Bozena and I laughed with tears of joy; we jumped up and down like little kids screaming, "Yes! Yes! Yes!" It was a great night and we hit the publicity jackpot with a ton of TV coverage over the next few days.

With the hokum and hype over, it was time for Magicopolis to sink or swim in the strange and muddy waters of Santa Monica. There are many people, not just youngsters, who, usually confined to TV, computer, and movie screens, have never seen a live stage performance of any kind, let alone a magic show. And one cannot fully experience the art and craft of magic through any electronic medium, as can be done with comedy, music, or drama. A woman floating on screen just isn't the same as when you experience that phenomenon live and in person. Yet in Los Angeles, as with most venues outside of a few exceptions in Vegas and New York, the average amusement seeker is not used to paying hard-earned cash to see a magic show.

Penn & Teller on stage at Magicopolis opening night.

The opening night media support was overwhelming, but a groundbreaking ceremony attendee who was a journalist from the trendy monthly, *Buzz Magazine*, was quoted as saying, "It is needless for me to write about Magicopolis, in all probability the place will be out of business before the end of the year." That was back in March 1998. Since then we've had the good fortune to parlay our minimal talent into a long run and have been continuously presenting shows at Magicopolis right up until today in 2015. It was *Buzz Magazine* that filed for bankruptcy and went out of business before the end of that year. The magazine's June 1998 issue was Buzz's last.

Almost everyone, I imagine, has a year that seems peculiarly his own in memory, a year enshrined where fireworks ever explode. My year was 1997–1998, during which time I experienced a feeling of self-importance, which I never again possessed.

I'VE GOT THE SHOW
RIGHT HERE

Were you to attend a performance at Magicopolis tonight, it's likely you'd witness the latest and greatest version of the ever-evolving production, *Escape Reality*, with Steve Spill and Bozena Wrobel—a magical mystery tour de force of sleight of hand, illusions, levitation, mind reading, disappearances, and a nail-biting Houdini-inspired escape. The show is seasoned with hilarity and danger, and without any video walls, smoke machines, lasers, pyrotechnics, or tits-and-feathers dancers.

Building that show, or any show for that matter, was like building a cruise ship—until you get it in the ocean you can't tell if it's the *QE2*, or the *Titanic*. For some reason, I remember captaining my first creative ships, actually rowboats—the Highdini act and my Castle close-up show—more vividly in some ways than the collaborative construction of Escape Reality, even though our long-running Magicopolis ocean liner is superior in every way. Perhaps I dwell on those early vessels, which seem so small and obscure, because those efforts were the birth of the bread-and-butter philosophy that has been woven into the fabric of my career. Namely, that magic is a vehicle that must deliver some presentational content besides the trick itself.

Before Bozena, as a solo performer, I focused mainly on comedy. The Bozena collaboration added a female actor/writer's skill set to the mix. She had ideas, a deep knowledge of scene construction, and an expert capability of playing any character imagined. Bozena embodies the lives of beings with which I can interact—vampires, séance mediums, or even a horny man. The only character I can credibly play is an embellished version of myself.

Me about to say something stupid in front of both Bozena and Magicopolis.

Audiences accept the fact that women are often sawed in two or otherwise theatrically victimized in magic shows. We wanted to do that sort of trick where instead of a woman it was a man, me, that endured some torture. At the time, a magician in Texas offered to build and sell a copy of his then newly invented illusion that looked like this—a woman stood in a box with an open front so you could see her standing there. When the magician cranked some handles the top of the box lowered, the bottom heightened, and the girl's head and feet drew closer together. This contin-ued until she became compressed to less than 18 inches in length.

We gave my measurements over the phone and had him build the special box so that I, a man, presumably could fit in it. We wrote a very funny sketch, The Runaway Groom, as a way of presenting this clever trick. When the prop arrived from Texas I could not fit inside, but, of course, Bozena could. Instead of having the thing re-built, we channeled our disappointment and anger into humor, and a new, funnier spin on our sketch sprang to life. Sometimes dealing with adverse situations brings something better than originally envisioned. That's what happened here when we decided to switch roles.

Besides the broad hilarity of it all, the unforeseen cool thing about me playing the bride and Bozena acting as the groom is that the role reversal actually better presents the qualities of a cheating macho groom and a manipulative abandoned bride, in a more exaggerated, poignant, expressive way, than if we did the bit as originally intended. Plus it's much funnier.

The plot is introduced on stage like this: "I'd like you to imagine the worst day in a young beautiful woman's life. It's her wedding day, and her husband-to-be fails to show up at the ceremony. He leaves her standing at the alter." On cue, in unison, the entire audience always sighs a very audible "aaahhh" sort of sound. "You've heard of the Runaway Bride. Now it's time to meet The Runaway Groom."

I left the stage and Bozena, snappily dressed as a man with an open shirt exposing a hairy chest jangling with gold chains, snuck out and started flirting with a woman in the audience.

"What's cookin' good lookin'? My name is Harry— Harry Chest." She/he improvises and not only gets the woman's name, but often her phone number, email address, zodiac sign, and location for a first date as well—until I burst onto the scene, dressed in full drag bride regalia, including a beautiful wedding dress, jewelry, bouquet, and my usual goatee.

"I see you there, trying to pick up on that smoking hot hottie hotsy totsy...you miserable pig!" After I smack the groom with my bouquet and turn away in an indignant pose, my fiancé says, "Good to see you baby." I, in drag, matter-of-factly respond, "I don't think Tootsie or Mrs. Doubtfire had to put up with this sort of Crying Game..."

"Oh come on baby, be my bride, give me a little kiss..."

"I remained celibate for you! I mean, except for Brad Pitt and Larry King. Oh, that Larry, I love getting tangled in his suspenders..."

"You betrayed me?"

"The thing to remember is that I stood back there waiting for you, with all my friends and family..." As I gestured with my bouquet, I became distracted by it. "Hey, these smell pretty good. Well, if I can't get lucky, maybe someone else will."

I toss the bouquet into the audience. If a woman catches it, I say, "Hand it to a man, I don't go that way." If a boy catches it, I ask, "What do you think I am, a cougar?" One way or another, after various adlibs, the bouquet ends up with a man in the audience, usually a handsome one. "Hey, what's your name, you big strapping stud? He's very cute, look at the muscles on that fella."

Acting jealous, my groom flexed and bragged, "I've got big muscles too, but hey buddy, do you have a hairy chest? Come on, show us your carpet of pleasure." They cried out from the audience egging him on, and the guy was coaxed into taking off his shirt as the crowd cheered.

"I think he waxes...I like the pierced nipple...He's very cute."

"Well if you like him so much, why don't you marry him?"

I stroked my hair, batted my eyelashes, and made an innocent but seductive sort of pose, "Do you think he really likes me?" Then I pulled up my dress to show a little leg, "Oh come on baby, you know you want it."

Suddenly I snapped out of it and got back to the issue at hand, "The thing to remember..." speaking to my groom, "...is that I stood back there waiting for you..." I look at the audience, "I don't know if we should whip him, beat him, kiss him, or squish him? I think we ought to squish him!" As I say, "squish him!" two things happen—the curtains opened to reveal the torturous squishing box, and I reach into my bra and take out my falsies, actually a pair of maracas. I shake the maracas to the beat of my chant, "squish him, squish him, squish him..." the audience joins in, "squish him, squish him, squish him," and my groom is forced into the box.

I put the maracas back in my bra, "They just don't shake like they used to," and start the squishing process, as my

191

groom gets smaller and smaller. In sheer agony, we hear the apologetic pleas for mercy:

"Please don't squish me. Please don't squish me. You know I love you baby. It wasn't my fault..."

"Oh yeah? What kind of lame excuse do you have for not showing up?"

"There was an earthquake...a horrible flood...my car ran outta gas..."

"But the limo was supposed to pick you up."

The squish completed, Harry's head just a few inches above his feet, the groom shouts, "My feet don't smell so good." The box is turned around so the audience can see our squishee from every angle. I scream, "Take a good look Harry. I want you to see how it feels to be embarrassed in front of your friends and family. What do you have to say for yourself now, little man?"

"I feel so small."

"I think I'm gonna take the limo to Vegas!"

The curtains close and the bit is over.

While developing our show, we argued about almost every bit and piece along the way until we came to agreement. If a disagreement on any certain trick, routine, or dialogue wasn't settled, we got rid of it. This wasn't some rule of thumb or even discussed; that's just how we did and continue to do it. Those opinions often changed to confront obstacles, logistic or otherwise, and we made incremental changes or dumped whole bits, as we saw fit. Debating with ourselves, and each other, the arguments over creative differences made us really commit.

With the benefit of audience feedback, after each performance we'd replay the show in our heads, figuring how to make it better and better. We spent day after day in the theater cutting and fixing and changing and switching. Our best work is about more than floating ladies, mind reading, and sleight of hand. It's as much about what we want to say as the tricks themselves. It is about us, our lives, and our feelings. Many of the show's best moments were initially improvised on stage.

Bozena and I are as synchronized as the parts in a watch. When either of us goes off script and does or says something different, we can follow each other without missing a beat. And whenever we hit a perfect moment the audience feels it. We also work with the reality of the moment. In a play, if a light suddenly goes dead or someone throws up in the audience, the actors keep doing the script. When things out of the ordinary arise during our show, we use them, respond to them, and weave them into our presentation. Sometimes, not knowing what's going to happen next is a ton of fun.

Bozena and I killing time between shows.

This chapter wouldn't be complete without an example of one of the solo pieces we each perform in the show. First up, my bit with three leaves. I'm fond of this one more for what it is about than what it is.

As I explain to the audience, "I'm twelve years old and obsessed with card tricks. The problem is that I'm not very good, and the only way I can get good is by doing a bunch of shows. My neighbor tells me that there's a talent show every Sunday in Topanga Canyon at the Theatricum Botanicum. So I call up, say I'm twelve years old and would like to do card tricks. The guy says, 'Not interested!' and hangs up.

"My neighbor tells me, 'If they think a few people might come see you do the show, maybe they'll put you on.' So at my request, friends start calling, 'When is Magic Steve going to be appearing?' The guy gets pestered, worn down, and gives me an audition. I hitchhike up to Topanga Canyon. The Theatricum Botanicum is an outdoor wooden stage, eaten by woodpeckers. It's surrounded by a jungle of plants and trees. I'm soaking up the vibe.

"Oh my gosh, what an idiot I am! I left my deck of cards in the car that picked me up hitchhiking, and this is gonna be my first and worst audition ever. An angry poet and a folk singer are also waiting to audition. This was 1967, and there were a lot of angry poets and folk singers. They say if you remember the sixties you weren't there. I was there. Peace, love, ban the bomb. So while I'm waiting for my turn, I decide I'm going to do a card trick with some leaves I picked up.

"I had, one, two, three leaves..." I showed three large banana tree leaves. "I take away one leaf..." I dropped one on the floor, "...and I still have one, two, three, leaves." Again I counted the leaves slowly, and there were still three. "The theater director jumped up, pumped his fist into the air, and screamed, 'Right on Dude!'

"I started to explain how I lost my cards, I knew this probably wouldn't work, and the guy says, 'No kid, that was kinda eccentric, how does that go again?' I threw in an 'I can dig it,' and said, I have one, two, three leaves, this time I take away not one, but two leaves..." I dropped two leaves on the floor. "And I still have one, two, three leaves.

"The theater director jumped up, pumped his fist into the air, and screamed 'Right on dude!' In fact, everyone, jump up, pump your fist in the air and scream, 'Right on dude!'" Most everyone in the audience did it, I threw in another "I can dig it," and continued, "He says, 'This gets better every time I see it.' So I go with it again, clearly counting and showing three single and separate large banana tree leaves. This time I take away, not one, not two, but three, four, five, six, seven..." For the finish, one at a time, I threw away twenty-nine leaves. "The theater director jumped up, pumped his fist into the air, and screamed..." At this point everyone in the crowd with a brain jumped up, pumped their fist in the air, and screamed at the top of their lungs, "Right on dude!" Then I threw in a final, "I can dig it!"

If the leaves routine has a familiar ring to it, that's because of Senator Crandall. You may remember him earlier in the book as the fellow who did The Six Card Repeat Trick at the Magic Castle back in the sixties. That was part of the inspiration for the leaves.

As for Bozena's solo bits, here's one of my favorites that she does: She lights a candle, then unravels a single strand of thread from a spool. As she stretches the thread between her outstretched hands, she says, "Over the course of one's life we are all bound to experience..." using the candle flame, she cuts the thread in two "...a broken heart..." another cut, "...disappointment..." another cut, "...sickness or..." another cut, "depression..."

The multiple pieces of thread are rolled between her fingertips, "...and finding something funny or entertaining under those painful conditions is good. If you can laugh even while you feel pain, there's hope. If you can rediscover laughter and forget your problems for a while..." She blew on the rolled pieces, which instantly and visually restored back to their original state. Bozena again unraveled the thread between her outstretched hands accompanied by her final thoughtful words, "...then you are on the road to being whole again."

Countless times, I've been told stories of those who have dealt or are dealing with life's hard knocks that took the words Bozena shared in her thread bit to heart. More than a few have said it's their favorite part of our performance. I had the notion that more often than not people liked going to our show to forget their problems rather than be reminded of life's big issues, but with this trick of Bozena's they get both.

One night a guy had his head in his lap for the entire show. Even though I always improvise, I didn't question it, because the girl with him seemed to be emoting a "What's wrong with you baby?" sort of sympathy that made me think the guy was probably ill. Who knew? Maybe he ate some bad clams. As you know, my lifelong custom after every show is to do the meet and greet with the audience. As per the request of his female counterpart, the "head in the lap" guy snapped a photo of me and his girl, before saying, "I'm happy Suzy had a good time, but I'm not allowed to watch magic..."

I kidded, "Not a problem as long as you buy a ticket."

"It's not a joke."

I couldn't tell if this guy was putting me on, "What do you mean, you're not allowed? Not even card tricks?"

"The Ace of Spades is the death card and the Queen of Hearts brings to mind a girl who was drowned. Those are cardboard instruments of the devil and witchcraft is a violation of Baptist law."

"I do tricks, not witchcraft, right?"

"Well, it's not just that," he said. "There is a Baptist prohibition of doing anything that 'looks' like you're violating Baptist law, for fear that you may lead others down your rocky path. Then of course, there is the issue of lying, which is a rather cowardly thing to do. Can you honestly say you told the whole truth, and nothing but the truth, during the entire show?"

Just for fun I changed the subject. "Do you believe in pre-marital sex?"

"Never mind!"
"I take that to mean definitely yes!"
"No, it does not mean yes!"

TABLE OF TERROR

There is one person associated with the world of magic more than any other in the eyes of the public, and that man is, of course, Harry Houdini. Dead for decades, yet still the most Googled magician, kids do book reports on him; people use phrases like, "doing a Houdini;" his name is synonymous with the word "magic;" he's been immortalized in numerous stage productions, TV specials, and feature films; and plenty of new Houdini projects are always in the works. Like Elvis or Michael Jackson, he seems to be as active now, or more so, than he was when he was alive.

At Magicopolis we close almost every show with a wonderfully terrifying experience that is a tribute to the man who built his career in a branch of our craft known as escapology. Houdini's feats helped to define the basic repertoire of escapology, including escapes from handcuffs, chains, ropes, mailbags, beer barrels, and prison cells.

The most dramatic of these kinds of stunts are the ones where the magician is trapped in a dangerous situation and required to escape from it or suffer a fate of certain doom. Like the upside-down straitjacket escape where the magician is suspended high in the air from a burning rope, or underwater escapes where the threat of drowning exists. Theatrically speaking, the most effective of these types of tricks are the ones where it appears that the escape has gone wrong, giving the audience the impression the performer must have been killed or badly injured. If the audience happens to love the magician, when he reappears unharmed they can be particularly generous with their applause.

Danger is a strong attraction for the public. Everyone likes to court death a little, without getting too near it, even if they only do it vicariously by watching films or TV or playing video games. At Magicopolis, we cater to this interest with the Table of Terror. The apparatus consists of a metal table with an array of threatening sharpened steel spikes suspended above it. The basic premise is that the performer, yours truly, is restrained on the table and must escape before the spikes are released and allowed to fall.

Originally known as The Death of Coira, it was created by magician Walter Jeans, who lived 1877 to 1942, and no, neither he nor Coira died doing it. The more modern incarnation of the trick was refined and updated in my lifetime by magician Andre Kole, a prolific inventor of illusions performed by some of the greatest in our field. I contacted him in an effort to either buy his prop, as the word was he was no longer using it, or get permission to use his design and methodology to have my own version built.

As touched upon elsewhere in this book, the world of magicians is small, and when someone develops a routine or unique apparatus, it is only fair, a professional courtesy, and ethical, to get their permission to build upon their work, whether it is a sleight of hand trick or a big stage illusion. With a large potentially dangerous prop like this one, there is also a big advantage in having the counsel of someone who has performed it and developed certain secret features and mechanical innovations. The design and construction of my Table of Terror was handled by precision craftsman William Kennedy, a well-known illusion builder who specializes in dependable metal fabrications, to whom Kole referred me as being the best choice for my needs.

Before sharing the harrowing situation I survived performing the Table of Terror on one fateful night back in 2009, I ask your indulgence while I attempt to paint a picture of what it would be like if you had been in the audience for a typical thrilling performance of this funny, scary, and dangerous presentation. I stood on a dark stage, in a small pool of light, and said...

"Harry Houdini died nearly nine decades ago, and to this day he is still the most famous magician in the world. He was not only a great magician, but also invented a whole new type of magic, escapology, and it was always his policy to close his show with a dramatic death-defying escape...and it was always something so unbelievably daring that no one would have the nerve to try it.

"Back in 1926, the year Houdini died, he was closing his show with the Water Torture Cell, where he was secured upside down in a glass tank filled with water. At the time, plans were underway for a new escape, which he called the Table of Terror. That's the one we're going to close our show with. Quick warning, if you're easily frightened or have a weak heart, now is the time to leave. That said, it's our pleasure to close the show with the...TABLE OF TERROR!"

On the word "TERROR!" the curtains parted, there was a dramatic stark shadowy shift in the lighting, and eerie music was heard as a massive steel structure came into focus. Assistants pushed forward the one-ton device with dozens of spikes that hung above a metal table with holes in it that matched the layout of the spikes.

"Thirty-nine sharpened steel spikes that can pierce concrete yet remain sharp enough to perform delicate eye surgery! We're going to have someone from the audience take a close look at the items we'll be using for this escape..."

A man was invited on stage to take a close-up view of the equipment. "I'd like you to touch the point of any of the spikes, to verify that they are real, they're metal, they're pointed, they're not rubber or collapsible...Now sir, for safety reasons, please stand way away. Speaking of safeties, we're going to take the safeties out right now..." Assistants removed some short steel bars that had prevented the spikes from dropping; now the spikes were held in place by a long thick rope. Dark blue light reflected off the metal, giving the contraption a cold, menacing look.

"Right now the spikes are only about halfway up; when they are all the way at the top, fifteen feet up, and they're released, the load is five thousand pounds. This is only about half way, but it's enough to give you the idea." The spikes were allowed to fall. When they hit the table the loud metal on metal crash was deafening, the music cranked up a few notches, and at that instant, the lighting turned blood-red. After their fall, the solid two-inch-thick, two-foot-long steel spikes could clearly be seen protruding through the bottom of the table and a few audience members jumped from their seats and ran from the theater.

"In a moment the spikes are going to be at the top; I am going to be secured to the bed of this device. We have a safety rope that's going to hold the spikes in place. The safety rope is going to be lit on fire." As I spoke the spikes were slowly hoisted fifteen feet up, and a mom with two kids got up and moved quickly for the exit. In their hearts, they knew this was just another magic trick in a magic show, but still, they felt there was a possibility something could go wrong, that I might die a horrific death, impaled by thirty-nine sharpened steel spikes with great amounts of blood spurting from the gaping wounds.

"The safety rope is not an ordinary fiber rope like the type we're hoisting the spikes with. It's a coiled cloth rope made out of burlap. It's been soaked in lighter fluid, scored with a knife, and we've burned it. And when we light it again, it will take one to three minutes to burn through. That's how long I'll have to make this escape...

"I should tell you, burning burlap is an inexact science. The safety rope has snapped prematurely in the past. Kind of funny, a six-year-old told me it would be much scarier if the spikes were dipped in poison! If I perish, I'd like it to be said I expired heroically and in the line of duty."

Bozena appeared with a table covered with various restraints, including manacles, leg irons, chains, and padlocks, and our volunteer was asked to inspect each of these as they were put to use. "If you would, first we'd like you to take a look at the manacles; make sure the bar is solid, the chains are welded on there..." As Bozena fitted the manacles around my wrists, I instructed, "Make sure the small padlocks operate properly, that they can't be opened without the key..." The small padlocks were locked into the loops of chain connected to the manacles, further tightly securing my wrists together.

"Next I'd like you to take a close look at the leg irons, pull on them, make sure they're solid and don't come apart..." As the restraints locked my feet together, I explained, "Sometimes these are called ankle hobblers; they're the same type you'd find at...home in any bedroom." Several more large padlocks and chains were inspected, then, flat on my back, my shackled hands and feet were padlocked to the metal table, and a final padlock and chain secured my waist.

A very small sheer translucent cloth, barely large enough to shield my body from the audience, was hung. Because of the extremely bright back lighting, everyone could see my silhouetted shadow and subsequent struggle to escape before the spikes fell. Everything above and below me was in plain view. The Led Zeppelin song "Rock & Roll" was cranked up to a skull-rattling volume as the safety rope was lit on fire. The flames erupted and curled upward. Those in the front row could feel the heat from the red and orange flames that burned like the fires of hell.

I had told the audience it would take one to three minutes to make my escape. Less than a minute elapsed when it was apparent I had one hand free. Then, suddenly, the safety rope unexpectedly snapped and the spikes crashed down on the table. It was obvious I had not completed the escape. Some men, women, and children screamed a continuous, high-pitched, shrill sound of terror. One woman quickly rose in horror from her seat and spilled her drink on the woman in front of her, who paid no attention whatsoever because she thought she had wet her pants in fright. The small piece of cloth fell away; instead of being shish-kabobbed to death, there I was standing on top of the spikes—alive, well, and happy to receive some enthusiastic applause.

That, of course, was all part of the show. Now to the unintended harrowing Table of Terror situation, which I luckily survived one fateful night back in 2009. At the time, many of our fans were criminals, gang members, malcontents, natural enemies of all law and order except their own. Magicopolis was involved with a community service program that enabled certain juvenile detention center and probation camp residents to take field trips to various cultural events, exposing them to new types of music, theater, and art. The purpose of the program was to interest these kid convicts in something other than committing felonies, or perhaps to make juvenile delinquents into jubilant delinquents, but not all delinquents are ripe for rehabilitation.

Bozena relaxing on the Table of Terror.

It was a Friday night. So there I am, chained, Zep blasting, rope blazing, while in the gentlemen's powder room—just for kicks—one of the teenage outlaws, who had been unsupervised for a fraction of a second, stood on a toilet testing a ceiling fire sprinkler heat sensor with a lit match. Our fire alarm system was up to code. In that fraction of an instant, there was a wailing siren, flashing lights, and an intimidating automated voice evacuation system demanding that everyone leave the building; then there were drops of rain, clouds of water, wet stage lights flashing showers of sparks, and audience members bolting for the exits. They evacuated in droves.

The all-star staff determined there was no fire, turned off the sprinklers, canceled a fire department response. When I escaped, the theater was less than a third full, and that remaining handful of hardy souls gave me a standing ovation. Actually, I'm not sure if it was a standing ovation, or if they were just a tad behind the others in jumping up to run for their lives.

DOUBT OF THE BENEFIT

Charity starts at home, but here in Los Angeles every night, in every hotel ballroom in town, some professional philanthropist or some popular disease is being honored. Many of these events are hosted by celebrities to assure a sellout; none really need to hire a magician, but some do. I have appeared at dozens of benefits and charity affairs and I will continue doing it, not only for pay. When you are a magician, a lot of charitable groups, civic organizations, and government agencies ask you to donate your time to do shows for them—like the Red Cross ladies who are always ready to offer themselves for charity. Sometimes I'll do those for nothing to support organizations I'm fond of.

At Magicopolis, we also have been, and continue to be, big supporters of the Children's Hospital Los Angeles Blood Drive. Now more than ever, we are encouraging people to donate a pint of blood and get a free ticket to our show. Thousands have done it, and only once we had a problem— someone who didn't think I was a very good magician asked for his blood back.

It was the fall of 2011 when I received a phone call from someone in New York offering me a job at a benefit to be held just minutes from Magicopolis, in Santa Monica. The pleasant voice on the phone said, in part, "This is a small boutique event and it's important you look very 'magishinee' like you do in your pictures on the Magicopolis website."

I e-signed an agreement, and the next day I received a FedEx with payment in full and details of the event. I deposited the check but took only a quick glance at the details, since the show date was several weeks away. On the appointed day at 10:00 a.m. I arrived at a small children's bookstore on Montana Avenue. The walls were decorated with original artwork and prints from books like *Stuart Little, Charlotte's Web*, Peanuts comics, and all things Seuss.

I was greeted warmly by a woman from the public relations firm that hired me. The lady was sweet and apologetic when she said, "We may not need you, but if we do, it will only be as background eye candy." I wasn't sure what she meant, but I said something to the effect of "no worries" and found a quiet corner to wait and see what would happen. Also on site were three cameramen with three corresponding entertainment news reporters.

Shortly thereafter about ten kids and their moms appeared. They were seated on the floor in front of a large stuffed chair and everyone was given a gift bag. The kids were delighted with little teddy bears, cookies, and lollipops. The mom's swag bags had soap, perfume, and makeup samples.

Next a world famous model/television host appeared. I don't remember her name because a confidentiality clause forbids my disclosure of her name and I don't want to be sued. I'll call her "Star." Star sat comfortably in the large stuffed chair. The children were attentive and the quiet was deafening. Then the lights became very bright and the cameras started to roll. Star picked up a copy of *Cat in the Hat* and started reading aloud...

And then, on cue, in the middle of the first line, she stopped reading, the lights went down, the cameras stopped rolling, and the kids and moms were excused. Total time lapse was about five minutes.

The remaining people and equipment were rearranged and the reporters each had a brief on-camera chat with Star. And that was it. The entire ordeal, from start to finish, was over and done in under an hour. Had I been needed, I'm told they would have gotten a shot or two of me doing some tricks for the kids.

This pretend benefit, or whatever it was supposed to be, was in reality just a publicity stunt that used the cause as a hook to put the eyes of the nation on Star. That evening on television, here's how the entertainment programs covered the event:

Anchor boldly announces: "Star champions overcoming childhood illiteracy worldwide at a benefit in Santa Monica, California. For more on this story here's our on-location field reporter…"

Upbeat music played as we saw exterior/interior shots of the cute kid's bookstore and close-ups of intrigued children and moms. Reporter: "I'm at a glorious family-friendly benefit here in this cute kid's bookstore where world famous model/television host Star is taking time out of her busy schedule to raise awareness for a cause that's close to her heart…"

Footage of Star reading aloud, before they cut to the reporter, who was dripping with TV host affection: "It's all about the kids, isn't it Star?"

Star pursed her lips while looking deeply into the camera lens and answered: "That's right. It's all about kids overcoming illiteracy because learning to read is critical to a child's success."

Reporter: "I couldn't agree more Star, and I must say that when I watched you reading to those kids you were absolutely glowing."

Star: "That's partly because of my new skin care line coming to abc or xyz boutiques this spring. And the fine folks at def stores would think it's a crime if I didn't let all my fans know that this polka dot outfit I'm wearing, along with all Star styles, fashions, accessories—including my new signature shoes and sunglasses—are available right now at def stores worldwide."

Cut to anchor: "Thanks for that on-location report. Be sure to watch Star's hit show on the xyz network every Tuesday at 9:00 p.m. We'll be back after this…"

I guess the lesson to be learned here is that it feels good helping children. I wished Star well, not only on the overcoming illiteracy project, but also in the sufficient attainment of future publicity—at least as much publicity as is necessary to hire me to appear at another family-friendly benefit.

BRUSHES WITH GREATNESS

I love being in the orbit of great personalities, and through Magicopolis I've met Sylvester Stallone, John Malkovich, Danny DeVito, Billy Bob Thornton, and many others. Starting on our opening night in 1998, I kept a list of accomplished recognized people who visited. When the list reached the one hundred mark, I stopped keeping track. It's a great perk meeting famous people you admire and I used to ask many of them to sign their name on a wall in the theater.

Next to Meg Ryan's signature, Arsenio Hall signed and wrote "Ooohh." Under David Bowie's name, Albert Brooks quipped, "I'm with David." Kevin Sorbo, who at the time was playing Hercules on TV, signed his name very tiny, while Arianna Huffington's signature is just plain huge. "Boo" is what Stephen King wrote above his autograph.

After each performance, I always shake hands or chat with those who care to, and some snap their photo with me. Around 2008, after the show I was chatting with comedian Chris Rock and someone on our staff took a picture. The photo of Chris and me was hung on the wall, and it didn't go unnoticed. Before Chris, for some reason it never occurred to me to have a camera handy so I could get photos with some of the luminaries that cross our path.

Now I proudly hang dozens of celebrity photos on our wall, and post many of them on our website. It is effective marketing, plain and simple. I believe when potential patrons see the photos it adds a "wow" factor that pushes some who might not otherwise buy a ticket, to do so. In a sense it's like those photos are vouching for Magicopolis, like a multi-million-dollar ad campaign.

I think they think, "If Jack Black thinks Magicopolis is cool, then it is cool." Or "That magician is standing beside John C. Reilly. Reilly is talented so that magician must be talented," or "I like Neil Patrick Harris, so I like Magic."

The photos seem to make people know me in a second-hand fashion. They sense Sting and I are good friends, and that in turn makes me a friend of theirs. They've been listening to his music for years, they stress how much he means to them, and some even ask me to give Sting their regards.

The art and craft of magic does have its share of show-biz types who are big fans, and some, like Neil Patrick Harris, Steve Martin, Woody Allen, Arsenio Hall, and Jason Alexander, are actually skilled magicians themselves.

Most of my celebrity encounters are a mere exchange of the cliché phrase "love your work," a quick hello, perhaps a famous smile and a handshake, or all of the above.

Though I've entertained celebrities from Jamie Lee Curtis to Meg Ryan, one of my most memorable stories is with Stephen King. To coincide with the release of his novel *Bag of Bones*, the monarch horror writer headlined a private event at Magicopolis for a select audience of book reviewers and retailers. He read aloud a story especially penned for the occasion, answered questions, and gave everyone a signed book. What's not to like?

This was a goodwill-type gathering sponsored by King's publisher and retailer Borders Books. King and his entourage of three were gathered in my dressing room. I was slightly acquainted with the Borders dude—he was a friend of a friend, and the guy who hooked up this deal—and the other two were publisher's reps.

Introductions were made. In the background we heard the audience filing into the theater along with some audience-filing-into-the-theater-type music. As the five of us chatted, King lit a cigarette.

Indoor smoking has never been allowed at Magicopolis, but since this was STEPHEN KING, the guy who sold hundreds of millions of books, many of which had been made into blockbuster movies, perhaps the most successful author ever, out of respect and admiration, I didn't say anything and neither did anyone else.

But I felt certain we were all thinking about it when the Borders guy asked playfully, "Hey Spill, why don't you show us some magic?" I replied, "Of course, happy to honor your request." Before responding I was already thinking about doing the vanishing cigarette trick.

Had I done that trick, I would have borrowed one of the men's jackets. They were all wearing coats and ties, except for King who was in a tee shirt and jeans. The lit cigarette would have been ground into the fabric of the coat. Smoke would have curled upward and I'd have said, "Don't worry— it's a smoking jacket, it could become a blazer." There would have been laughs, the cigarette would have vanished, the coat would have been returned unharmed, and everyone would have been amazed.

Could have, would have, didn't. Instead, at the exact moment I had finished the sentence, "Of course, happy to honor your request," there was a power outage—pitch-black darkness, music gone, and we heard an echoing collective sigh from the theater crowd.

Ten seconds later the power burst back on. Bright lights, background music, in the distance a cheer of relief from the audience. I instantly barked "ta da" at the same moment King screamed "wow," and the entourage of three gave me a brisk sitting ovation. I smiled. Six seconds passed. King finished his cigarette and lit another.

Another one of my most memorable celeb interactions via Magicopolis was with the one and only Rob Reiner. The first Reiner I met at Magicopolis was Carl. I'm a big *Dick Van Dyke Show* fan, and Carl shared some hilarious anecdotes about being the Emmy Award-winning creator of that series. Carl's son Rob is the first Reiner I saw in person, way back when I was part of a studio audience that witnessed the taping of an early *All in the Family* episode. That was Rob Reiner the Emmy Award–winning actor. Both Reiners are friendly, funny, and enormously talented writer/director/ actors.

The subject at hand is when Rob Reiner—the genius of an auteur behind some of the world's best-loved films like *Stand by Me, When Harry Met Sally, A Few Good Men, The Princess Bride, Misery,* and *This Is Spinal Tap*—brought his wife and kids to our show at Magicopolis.

One of the tricks I love to perform starts when I ask people that are wearing a ring on one of their fingers to raise their hands. I borrow a few of the most unique or unusual-looking rings available, and magically cause the rings to link together, then unlink, and return them unharmed to their owners.

The plot is the same as the classic Chinese Linking Rings. In the traditional trick, solid metal rings appear to link and unlink, pass through each other, and form a chain. The big difference between the classic and what I do is that the version I perform uses borrowed rings.

Some watching think the trick with borrowed rings might be done with magnets or thread, or that the people who loaned the rings are secret assistants. To assure the audience none of those things are true, it is essential to have each of the owners identify themselves and their rings and verify their rings are indeed linked to the others. Those ring owners' eyewitness testimonials are what convince the audience the illusion is real.

To get them to really emote I say things like, "Tell me Susan, do you see your ring there? And is it in fact linked onto the other rings? What do you think about that?"

At times spectators drop their jaws in awe and are speechless; it is great when the surprise delivers a big emotional impact like that, but it is not as dramatically satisfying to the audience as hearing them say out loud what they really think and feel.

Honest and credible remarks from independent audience members are what transform this trick into a miracle. As an intuitive director and performer, Rob perceived this instantly and when participating he improvised a lengthy dramatic testimonial. In fact, Rob gave an over-the-top virtuoso performance like none I've witnessed doing this trick either before or since.

Steve: "Rob, is that your ring linked on the chain?"

Rob: "Oh my God, yes! That definitely is my ring linked on the chain! That is fantastic! Steve! You have touched me in a very intimate way! That ring is a family heirloom, an antique, passed down to me through generations of Reiners! And now it's really linked! That's so unbelievable! I am getting goose bumps and breaking into a cold sweat! I'm so mind-boggled that I just peed my pants!"

It was uproariously hilarious. I laughed loud and hard. The audience went wild. Thank you, Rob.

And then there was Mort Sahl, the political comedian extraordinaire. He first impressed me over four decades ago, cracking jokes about current events on Hugh Hefner's TV show, *Playboy After Dark*. Mort was the first to record a comedy album, first comedian on the cover of *Time Magazine*, and today's wittiest and most irreverent politicos have followed in his footsteps.

Leading up to the 2004 presidential election Magicopolis hosted Entertaining Politics, a series of six Tuesday night political satire and commentary sessions. Nearly eighty years old at the time, Sahl kicked off the series on October 12, and his one-man concert of humor was arguably the best of the bunch. But it almost didn't happen.

Mort very politely introduced me to his wife and was escorted to his dressing room. I was visiting with guests in the bar when Mort's assistant sprinted in to ask where he could get a copy of *The New York Times*. I directed him to the

Promenade Newsstand around the corner. It was late in the day and the newsstand was sold out, so the assistant returned with a copy of the *Los Angeles Times* instead. No good.

As with most people who are brilliant, funny, and demanding, Mr. Mort Sahl was in his own world, operating from his own agenda. Mort's trademark had always been to appear on stage with that day's edition of *The New York Times*. Not the *Washington Post, USA Today*, or the *Los Angeles Times*. More than a prop, *The New York Times* was a ritual, a superstition, a good luck charm, a reassuring habit, and Mort wouldn't do the show without it.

It occurred to me that around the other corner and down the block, in the lobby of Lowes Hotel, there were always complimentary copies of all the national papers. My wife and I were/are members of the gym there, and Bozena was on the Stairmaster at that very moment. I gave her a call, but same as the newsstand, it was late in the day, and there was no *New York Times*.

But Bozena still came through. Residing outside the women's sauna was a lone front page of *The New York Times*. The clever assistant neatly folded that single page over the aforementioned copy of the *Los Angeles Times*, creating the impression of a complete New York edition. Mort appeared onstage with what he thought was a complete copy of *The New York Times* dated October 12, 2004.

The newspaper was rolled up and held in Mr. Sahl's fist. We in the audience couldn't tell if it was *The New York Times* or *The National Enquirer*. My guests and I kept waiting for him to open the paper, or at least refer to it. He never did. A few minutes into the show, Mort tossed the newspaper aside, and that was that.

Josh Brolin, the rugged, naturally charming Oscar nominee and son of actor James Brolin popped in one afternoon. We had just finished doing the show for a bunch of kids on a school field trip when Bozena greeted him and his girlfriend. She gave a personal Magicopolis tour and quickly arranged for me to entertain them with a little on-the-spot, close-up sleight of hand performance. Turns out, Brolin is a big fan of magic who hung onto my every word and stared at my hands incessantly. He was the fan and I was the star as he asked question after question. "How did you get started?" "How long did it take to learn that trick you just did?" "Do you believe in real magic?" Sometimes movie people look up to purveyors of live performance skills. At the time I had just embarked on my journey as a writer and told him he could find in depth answers to all his questions right here in this book.

First, let me state unequivocally, that like most others on planet earth, I accord Bob Dylan the status of best song-writer ever, bar none, triple exclamation point!!! So when Dylan walked into Magicopolis, to me it was a very big deal.

But let me start at the beginning. Bob's offspring, Jakob Dylan, an accomplished singer-songwriter in his own right, brought one of his sons to our show. The boy was apparently bitten by the magic bug and needed a fix. Not long after, Grandpa Bob made two visits to our magic shop with this particular grandson in tow, shopping for magic tricks.

To Bob's credit, on each visit he was very careful not to spoil the child. Methinks he might have gone a tad over-board. Whenever Little Houdini—I don't know the kid's name so I've nicknamed him Little Houdini, LH for short—points out a trick he wants Grandpa to buy, it goes some-thing like this...

LH: "I want the Color-Changing Hanky."

Dylan: "How much is it?"

Me: "Seven dollars."

Dylan: "Jeez LH, that's very expensive. Are you gonna really practice with it? Are the scarves gonna be an asset to your being? Are these made from real silk? What method was used to stitch the hems?"

It was a tradition for TV host, producer, and cultural icon Dick Clark to bring his kids' families from England and Arizona when they got together over the holidays every year at his place in nearby Malibu. He always acted like he was proud of me, beaming, glowing, when he'd attend the Magicopolis show. He'd look me in the eye and say nice things. Dick liked magic and magicians and always bought his grandkids tricks as gifts. Before he got sick he did a little magic himself with his Svengali Deck and Scotch & Soda coin trick.

Along with his two daughters and wife, Adam Sandler also attended our show. We hung during the intermission, and I appreciated him taking the time to visit. If I didn't know better, by the way he seemed impressed with my tricks, I would have assumed he'd never witnessed a magic show before.

By the time the performance resumed, a gaggle of paparazzi had assembled in front of Magicopolis. Not sure how these instantaneous papa-ratso things happen, but it does with very hot stars. They'll stay outside, but they're not shy about pressing their cameras right up against our lobby windows. One of the worst in memory was when at the peak of her *Alias* TV show fame, Jennifer Garner visited. Situations like that, and the Sandler one, necessitate undercover surreptitious back door exits.

When the show ended, simultaneous to the Sandlers' secret back alley departure, another photo opportunity arose out front. As the crowd was filing out, a very excited Adam fan ran from the theater and screamed out loud for everyone to hear, "I got it, I got it! I got Adam Sandler's Tootsie

Pop! Adam ate this!" What she held tightly in her hand, high above her head, and waved profusely, belonged in the garbage. It was a tiny dab of chocolate on the end of a little white stick. Who knows, maybe she made a bundle selling that sucker as an authentic memento on eBay?

Everyone knows Sara Gilbert as a star of the *Roseanne* TV series and as host/creator of *The Talk*. Sara's older sister, Melissa Gilbert, is also known from the *Little House on the Prairie* series and as an actor and director of TV movies. At a Magicopolis party/magic show thrown by Holly Robinson Peete, star of *21 Jump Street* and *Hangin' with Mr. Cooper*, and her husband, NFL quarterback Rodney Peete, host on *The Best Damn Sports Show* series, back in 2010, among the famous faces was a Gilbert. The Gilbert who I instantly recognized as Melissa Gilbert was, in fact, Sara Gilbert. Without knowing it, I'd confused Melissa and Sara Gilbert. After the fact, I was told, none of the guests was willing to point out my error because everyone found it so funny, for a reason I really don't find that funny, even now. I guess I'm no industry insider.

Apparently, growing up in showbiz, Sara lived in Melissa's shadow. Sara being called Melissa was a cross to bear when Melissa was a household name and Sara was just becoming known. Sara was famous as Melissa's little sister, but now Melissa was famous as Sara's older sister. The roles had reversed, Sara was now better known, yet here at Magicopolis, she was still being dogged by me repeatedly calling her Melissa—especially annoying I'm certain, coming from some smart ass hippie magician.

During a mind reading experiment I said, "Melissa, pick a magazine, any magazine. Okay, Melissa, open the magazine you selected to any page. Now, Melissa, concentrate on one word on that page. Melissa, stay focused, because Melissa, I'm going to attempt to read your mind..."

I guess I was really rubbing it in. In my defense, no one ever corrected me, including Sara Gilbert, but I suppose I should have known something was up. Every time I called Sara, Melissa, she would roll her eyes while the two Peetes and party howled with laughter. Everyone was in on this joke I kept milking, except me.

After the show a lot of photos were taken. I smiled dreamily when I asked, pleasantly, "Hey Melissa, can you snap one with me?" Everyone cracked up, and then, they all really busted a gut when she screamed, "My name is Sara not Melissa!"

I felt like a bonehead, "Why didn't you correct me when I first called you Melissa?" Sara immediately put me at ease, telling me she knew I was obviously not aware of my mistake, so I asked again, "Why didn't you say anything?" Her answer, "I just didn't want to spoil everyone's fun, but that last Melissa was the straw that broke the camel's back."

HOW JOAN RIVERS
GETS ME LAID

Late September 2013, I got a call from producers of the reality series, *Joan & Melissa: Joan Knows Best?* They said Penn Jillette had recommended me to play myself on a magic-themed episode that he and Teller would be appearing in. I love Penn & Teller and am a big Joan Rivers fan. So, without hesitation I told them yes.

Not long after that the details were set. Besides my two days on camera with Joan, Bozena was also booked for a day, the production would be renting some of my props, and Magicopolis was arranged as a location. Penn & Teller would be doing their bits at another location on another day. But as a special added bonus, in addition to Joan, Bozena and I would also be sharing scenes with both Melissa Rivers and Broadway star Marissa Jaret Winokur.

On the set of *Joan Knows Best?* with Bozena and Ms. Rivers.

About Joan. Joan Rivers, the legendary octogenarian comedy icon, was, on camera, a hilarious, screaming, yelling, cursing, extremely vain, self-deprecating, acerbic, ribald, egotistical personality who's politically incorrect in every way possible.

On camera, I played opposite her and she did a million takes as that character. Off camera she was kind, gracious, easygoing, and generous. When Joan Rivers was playing Joan Rivers, I don't think she was acting like herself; I think she was playing the character of Joan Rivers. Sorry to disappoint you.

Next, a quick word about entertainment shows that are referred to as "reality" programs. *Cops* is perhaps a close-to-reality program. Cameras follow real-life law enforcement officers and capture them during car chases, making arrests, and taking bribes. I think the singing and dancing competitions and "Got Talent" shows are a little less "real" than *Cops*. As far as I can tell, the least "real" of the "reality" genre are the type of shows I've been involved with, including *Epic Meal Empire*, about a chef obsessed with bacon and whisky; *Pit Boss*, the saga of a talent agency for little people who rescue abused pit bulls as a hobby; *Candidly Nicole*, showcasing Nicole Ritchie's feigned ineptitudes; and two Magicopolis reality test episodes for new TV series.

In each of these productions, same as Joan's show, a story with a beginning, middle, and end was conceived. There was an outline about what needed to happen in a predetermined number of scenes or short situations to move the story forward to its conclusion.

The outlines didn't have dialogue. Everything said was made up on the spot. Scenes were repeated as many as a dozen times, and new dialogue was improvised each time. Favorite moments from all the different takes were edited together into the needed scenes. The edited scenes were assembled to make the reality.

The Rivers magic episode story outline went as follows: Joan tells Penn that her first showbiz job was as a magician's assistant. Penn responds that he and Teller are performing a charity show at the Magic Castle. Wouldn't it be great if Joan brushed up on her magic skills and also did the show? It sounds fun and Joan tells Penn yes. But Joan was a magician's assistant back in 1948, was fired after only one performance, and remembers nothing.

Winokur is manipulated into co-starring in Joan's magic act. Joan persuades Steve to teach them some big tricks. Screw-ups occur, Winokur feels humiliated and insulted by Joan. Winokur quits. At the last minute Joan convinces Melissa to participate. Master Magicians Joan & Melissa are a hit at the Magic Castle charity show.

On our first day, Joan and her comedy writer friend Tony meet Steve at the Magicopolis magic shop. Joan's motive is to get Steve to teach her how to float people and saw them in half, so she can be a big hit at the magic charity show, but first she wants to ingratiate herself and see if Steve is the right one to work with.

So, instead of coming out and saying what she really wants, Joan gives a cover story. She tells Steve she's shopping for magic tricks to give her grandson Cooper for his birthday. Joan makes Steve show her every trick in the store ten times.

That's what happens for the next few hours. I demonstrate scores of tricks while Joan and Tony constantly chime in with wise cracks.

One such example is with the Money Maker trick. I insert a blank piece of paper into a little plastic machine, turn the knob, and out comes a real dollar bill.

Joan: "Bernie Madoff got 150 years for that."

Steve: "I hear if you can make it through the first 100 years, the last 50 are cake."

Tony: "I invested all my money in wrestling magazines."

Since Joan was starring on stage with Penn & Teller at a big charity show at the Magic Castle the next night, she requested that I teach her to float a lady, saw a woman in half, and perform a Houdini-like dangerous escape in the next twenty-four hours.

For a good part of an hour we improvised and tried to surprise each other. I had to bring my A game to keep up with Joan and Tony when it came to the adlibs.

The next day arrived, and Joan entered the theater with Winokur, who she intended to saw in half. Bozena taught Winokur how to be "sawn" while Steve instructed Joan on her part. Winokur got stuck in the sawing-in-half box. Joan and Winokur argued, and Winokur quit.

Not a ton of on-camera time for me on day two, more for Bozena. Mostly, we got to witness Winokur, who starred in the long-running Broadway hit *Hairspray*, in concert with Joan. Once the outlined conflict ensued, Joan was a devastating explosion of funny as only she can be. I do not remember exactly how many various weird and wonderful things the girls adlibbed to light the fuse to that explosion, but I think what follows was my favorite.

Bozena: The trick to the "sawing" is a combination of yoga and clever carpentry. Let me show you what you need to do with your body.

Winokur: Impossible for me, I'm the kinda girl that pulls a hamstring opening mail.

Joan: Don't be a cry baby. If you push hard enough, your knee will bend the other way.

Bozena and I staged a few rehearsal moments with Joan and Melissa for the camera. But mostly the four of us practiced two illusions off-camera, Joan making Melissa invisible, and Joan shrinking Melissa.

Both illusions are particularly tricky because two persons' actions need to be simultaneously performed and coordinated with precision or someone could get hurt. Both women were diligent in practicing and when we finished they were ready for their big performance at the Magic Castle. It was a satisfying end to a delightful day.

As you may have gathered, I am very fond of the Rivers girls. What Bozena and I witnessed of their chemistry and relationship was inspiring. After the goodbye and thank you, Joan took a humongous multi-jewel encrusted gold ring off her finger and gave it to Bozena as a gift. She said, "Bozena take this for good luck." Bozena was so happy. I got lucky.

The gift that keeps on giving.

Nowadays, I mention the humongous multi-jewel encrusted gold ring and she's in the mood. Like a soothing pleasant melody, Joan's words float through Bozena's mind with an intensity that brings back feelings from that special day. "Bozena take this for good luck." Déjà vu. Bozena is happy. I get lucky. It's positively Pavlovian. Thank you Joan.

BACKWARD

I had to slowly walk backwards through my memory, to write what's between the introduction and here. Now that that's done, to bookend this book's introduction, what's left to do is to write this . . .

Do magicians instantly recall every single show they've ever done? Maybe some do, but I sure don't. Certain performances I'll never forget doing, while others, for whatever reasons, don't come to mind. A high school friend whom I hadn't seen since 1973 was at Magicopolis the other night. She brought up the weekly teen showcases I performed at in the late sixties at Sir George's Royal Restaurant on Roscoe Boulevard in Canoga Park. I instantly remembered, but had forgotten not because those shows weren't exciting and interesting for me at the time, but they just weren't uppermost in my thoughts over forty years later. Were it not for the elephantine memory of my former classmate, those appearances may have escaped posterity.

For those who crave incidental facts, someone else reminded me about my performances at Six Flags Magic Mountain and Universal Studios Hollywood. Others remember me from a college show or an appearance at their company party, all of which I'd also forgotten. I'm certain there are many other forgotten shows.

One of the most important things to remember is that, like a lot of performers in my age group, over the decades and with many thousands of shows behind me, I've met thousands of people and simply can't remember them all. Oftentimes, I am out somewhere . . . where some guy greets me, and the dialogue goes like this:

"Hello Steve. Long time no see."

After an embarrassing moment, he follows up.

"Look . . ." he says, "you don't remember me, do you?"

"Let's see..." I reply, fumbling, "it was at..."

"Yeah, I thought you didn't remember."

"I've...uh...ah...your name is Chad...but you used to be taller and you took your mustache off. What a change!"

"My name is Nick."

"You changed your name too?!"

I hate to hurt anyone's feelings by admitting that meeting them made so little impression on me that I've no recollection of doing so, but lying about it is usually worse.

"You don't remember me, do you?"

"I can't believe I would have met a girl like you and forgotten about it."

"Fantasy Springs, 1995," she said.

It was an Indian casino near Palm Springs where I'd done a show.

"And I was one of the dancers."

"Of course you were, now I remember!" I lied.

"I had the operation six months ago."

I probably had seen her dancing, but as a boy dancer. Now he was a girl, and a gorgeous one at that with newly installed anatomical features.

Around 1978 I was with my old buddy Bob Sheets at a magic convention in Wichita, Kansas. Approaching us was a rising young teenage magician, who later became a Vegas star, named Lance Burton. I urgently whispered to Bob, "That guy coming toward us. I've met him at least a half-dozen times. I have a terrible time remembering names." "That is young Lance Burton," Bob told me. "Lance, how nice to see you," I said when we met a moment later. "How are you?" I turned to my longtime buddy then. "Lance I want you to...uh...ah...to meet...uh...my old friend... ah...umm..."

Sooo, you who are reading this, if we should ever cross paths, help me when we meet, tell me who you are, and how you know me, if you do. The jolt of your words may bring a revival of half-forgotten nouns, that is to say, a resurgence of persons, places, things, from long ago. A good place for us to bump into each other is at Magicopolis in Santa Monica, where you can enjoy a magical mystery tour de force of sleight-of-hand, illusions, levitation, mind reading, disappearances, and a nail-biting Houdini-inspired escape.

As a special bonus, when we meet, tell me you purchased this book, not that you borrowed, or stole it, or just read this blurb in a bookstore, and I'll feature you on stage as a star in my next show or write about you glowingly in my next publication—if I remember.